# Becoming the Parent You Are Called to Be

## Leonel Colón

*Parent's Initiative: Becoming the Parent You Are Called to Be*
Copyright 2018 by Leonel Colón

All rights reserved. No part of this book may be reproduced, stored in a retrieval system, or transmitted in any form or by any means-electronic, mechanical, photocopy, recording, or otherwise-without prior written permission of the copyright owner.

Unless otherwise indicated, all Scripture quotations are taken from the *Holy Bible,* New Living Translation, copyright © 1996, 2004, 2015 by Tyndale House Foundation. Used by permission of Tyndale House Publishers Inc., Carol Stream, Illinois 60188. All rights reserved.

Scripture marked (NIV) is taken from the Holy Bible, NEW INTERNATIONAL VERSION®, NIV® Copyright © 1973, 1978, 1984, 2011 by Biblica, Inc.® Used by permission. All rights reserved worldwide.

Scripture marked (KJV) is taken from the Holy Bible, King James Version, which is in public domain.

# About the Author

Leo and Rebekah Colón, along with their two children, Zane and Marsaylah, live in Mobile, Alabama, where they attend and faithfully serve at Praise Family Church as a family. Growing up with fathers for pastors, Leo and Rebekah have been involved in church ministry their entire lives and served in many different roles in the church with a focus on student ministry. They now look forward to speaking at church events, camps, conferences, Bible studies, schools, and community events all over the country. While serving in local church ministry, they recognized the need to partner with parents and help equip them to raise the future generations to be Christ-followers. They truly desire that all parents understand and believe that their children are a reward, as Psalm 127:3 says.

Leo can be contacted at leonelcolon@me.com. Find out more about Parent's Initiative at http://parentsinit.com.

www.ingramcontent.com/pod-product-compliance
Lightning Source LLC
Chambersburg PA
CBHW052308300426
44110CB00035B/2176

# Acknowledgments

I am blessed and honored to know so many people who have inspired and supported me for so many years. I feel grateful towards God first because of who He is, what He has done for me already, and what I know He will continue to do in my life. Every day I hope and pray to honor Him by seeking Him fully, loving Him deeply, and making a difference.

This book would still be saved on my computer if it weren't for my lovely wife, Rebekah, pushing me to get this out there. You are truly a blessing to me and our family. I love you so much and I count it a blessing to do life with you. To Zane and Marsaylah, I couldn't ask for better children because you both are so tenderhearted and loving and truly enjoy life. You put up with me and my shortcomings and truly do want to honor me and your mother.

This also would not be possible if it weren't for my parents. Thank you for raising me the way you did. At times I may have been difficult, and you probably think that you failed me in some ways. I want you to know that I appreciate everything you have done for me and I love you both dearly. To my sister: I love you and I am proud of you. I know I may not say it much, but you've been through a lot and I know God is not done with you yet.

I would also like to thank Praise Family Church. I served you as a team pastor for many years, and I truly appreciate the way you have embraced our family during our time of transition and now as a member of the family. Pastor Tom, thank you so much for always believing in me and being a spiritual father in my life. I will always be indebted to you for the way you supported me during a time when I felt transition coming.

For all of you who have kept us and this ministry in your prayers and have supported Parent's Initiative financially, thank you so much. We truly believe that God is going to allow this ministry to make a huge impact, and you all have played a role in that. More parents are going to be awakened to the role and responsibility they have, and a lot of homes and children will be changed by it as they take the initiative.

Finally, to my extended family, friends, ministry partners, and social media followers: Thank you! Thank you for your feedback, encouragement, love, support, and sharing this ministry with others.

- Leo Colón

This page is dedicated to those who contributed in a big way to see this book come about. I personally set out to run a twenty-seven mile trail run in March 2018 to raise funds for this project, and these individuals contributed in a big way. Thank you so much for your belief in us and for your contribution!

- Leo and Rebekah Colón

**Many thanks to:**
Ed & Lucy Potts
Danny & Samantha Alexander
Owen & Connie Reichert
Praise Family Church
Double Portion Ministries

# Contents

| | |
|---|---|
| Chapter 1: The Problem | 9 |
| Chapter 2: First Things First | 19 |
| Chapter 3: Warning Label | 27 |
| Chapter 4: My Life, Family, and Parents | 35 |
| Chapter 5: Parenting Today | 45 |
| Chapter 6: Being Too Passive | 55 |
| Chapter 7: Being Too Aggressive | 69 |
| Chapter 8: Relationships | 79 |
| Chapter 9: Entertainment | 93 |
| Chapter 10: Nonsense and Training | 107 |
| Chapter 11: Sex | 119 |
| Chapter 12: Neglecting Awareness | 131 |
| Chapter 13: Encouragement | 141 |

# Chapter 1: The Problem

"A mother is disgraced by an undisciplined child"
(Proverbs 29:15b).

It was 4 a.m. on a Thursday morning, but I was not sleeping. Instead I found myself in turmoil over what I had seen on social media the night before. It was only a couple of pictures of a female student on spring break, pictures taken in a beach condo. The young lady pictured was currently in our student ministry and only a junior in high school. She had so much potential and definitely had the hand of God on her life. I respected her for the things that she had had to deal with in the past due to some unfortunate events. There are few people in this world who would have handled her circumstances in the manner she did. But this was something else altogether.

The posted pictures really upset my wife and me a lot. They disturbed me so much that I almost cried. I found myself looking at them over and over again. I was hoping they weren't real. There was a part of me that just wanted to ignore them and not even acknowledge their existence.

I had tried so hard to reach out to this student and her parents, talking with them often. Even though I had invested a lot of time in this young lady, there was little change. Many times, it felt like my voice was not heard. And it wasn't just mine. My pastor and his wife tried to help her too. Our hearts had gone out to this student in particular because of her situation and the closeness of their family to our church and staff.

There was that other part of me that just wanted to e-mail her parents and let them know how disappointed I was in them. I was fed up and

## PARENT'S INITIATIVE

tired of fighting this battle. I felt like I was losing it—not just with this family, but with other families as well. The more I thought about contacting them, the more I felt like it wouldn't matter anyway. It would more than likely be another failed attempt, or they would just get upset and even leave the church. They would take my call as a personal attack on their child instead of an offer of help. I am sure they were beginning to think that we had it out for their daughter and their family when actually, and in all that time, we just wanted God's best for them. We did not want to tell them how to raise their daughter or control them in any way; instead, we had a genuine desire to set them up for success and not failure.

On one occasion, they had asked me specifically why something was being said to them and not to other families in the church who were dealing with the same thing. They didn't know that on several occasions, we had pulled other parents aside too. We just didn't publicize that. We were simply trying to help them and protect them from future harm to their daughter, themselves, and their family. It's sad that often when people are made aware of a problem, they want to deny the existence of it more than they want to accept it and deal with it. Many times, God uses someone else to bring problems to our attention. We can all be blind to what is happening around us.

Back to those pictures. In one, a guy was behind the girl I knew. He was fully clothed, had his hands behind his head, and his midsection was near her bottom. It seemed like they were dancing in a sexual manner. She was slightly bent over, wearing shorts that she really had no business wearing and a white shirt that you could easily see through. It seemed that she was wearing a bathing suit top under it, or it could have been her bra. She had her lips puckered up like she was about to kiss someone, and her fingers made the peace sign. There was another girl I didn't know in similar poses. She was facing this young lady and didn't seem much older.

The question I kept asking myself was: Why? I was really hurt. So many times I had preached messages on fleeing the appearance of evil, being careful about who your friends were, and the importance of purity

## THE PROBLEM

and representing Christ in your actions, the way you dress, being careful what you post on social media, and so much more. I had prayed for this young lady on several different occasions and had seen God really get ahold of her in many different settings: youth retreats, services, mission trips, and more. It was really hard to see her doing this now. Her parents had also heard sermon after sermon on the importance of family, the importance of protecting their home, and keeping their kids accountable.

Other pictures caught my attention as well. There was one of only guys and this girl. She was with a guy, and his arm was around her waist; I did not recognize him, but he seemed to be older than her. It really does not matter whether I knew the guy or not: it looked bad. He had no shirt on, and they seemed to be in a condo too. Another teenage guy in the background held a blue plastic cup up in the air. There was no telling what was in it. It could have been tropical punch for all I knew, but that's not where my mind went.

It was spring break. Every year during spring break, students who do not have a strong relationship with God and no adult supervision party and get into trouble. These were pictures with no explanations—just "SB 2013" (Spring Break 2013) on the caption for each one. There is no telling how many of our other students had seen them. They were displayed for all to see, so I am sure other parents and church members saw them as well.

In another picture, the two girls were bent down to their knees like catchers in a baseball game with their tongues sticking out. They both had their hands in the air showing the "bull" signal. That same guy from the first picture once again had his hands behind his head; this time, his midsection was behind the other girl's head.

Why do I take the time to write this out in detail? As a parent of a boy who is seven and a girl who just turned two, this greatly disturbed me. As a student pastor of almost ten years, it greatly disturbed me. As a thirty-something man, it greatly disturbed me to see these young girls in what seemed like a condo full of guys, posing in these ways. There is no telling what happened on that night. Pictures can only say so much and always allow the mind to think the worst.

## PARENT'S INITIATIVE

So, there I was at four in the morning, unable to sleep. I finally got out of bed. Suddenly a torrent of thoughts and questions about all this tumbled out of me. I could not shake how disturbed and upset I was.

Where on earth were the parents of all those students? Why did the parents of the girl I knew allow her to leave wearing clothes like that? Did her parents have any clue who the other girl was? Did they know that girl's parents and what they allowed her to do? Did she leave the presence of her parents dressed in a decent manner, only to change after she left? Did their parents really know where they were and who they were with? Why would this young lady even think that it was OK to post these pictures for all to see? Did she not realize that her mom would see them? Did she not realize how many others would too? Did she not care?

It is very possible that this young lady lied to her parents and that they had no clue what she had really intended. It is possible that she told them that she was just going to catch up with some friends and hang out. I am sure she did not give her mom a heads-up and say that she was going to a party, take some questionable pictures, and then post them on social media. It was more than likely just a stupid decision, and her parents are not really to blame for this whole situation. It was just another case of a student "being a teenager." Right?

### Before I Saw Those Pictures

It was a Wednesday night. God had been doing a lot in our student ministry and our church. Since it was spring break for our public schools, we had fewer students come that night. Our service began at seven p.m., and I was going over my message at five as I usually did before youth prayer at six to refresh my mind and make some changes if needed. As I sat in a meeting room in our church, I felt that God was saying that what I had prepared was not meant for that night. I went into "scramble mode" just to make sure I had a backup plan. I did not have peace to share what I had prepared and wanted to make sure that, in case I was wrong, I would at least have something ready.

# THE PROBLEM

Service began, and I knew that something was going to happen. God was doing something, and it was going to be awesome! We had a powerful move of God, and several students were crying, worshipping, and just in awe of His presence. New students came that night who had never been to our student ministry or church before. They also experienced the presence of God.

I realized two important things. First, it did not matter who showed up and who did not show up to a service. All that really mattered was that God was there. The second thing was the real reason for this book: and it will be a little harder to take in than the first. That first idea is more common knowledge, and I am sure that you have heard that more than once, especially if you were raised in church. The second reason hit me because I am a parent.

I was sitting in the back of our student ministry sanctuary on a bench. We had just dismissed our students, but we had our student worship leader stay behind and continue to lead worship. We probably had a handful of students who continued to worship. I was praying, just sitting there thinking about the service we'd just had, and it hit me. I was talking to God about some things that I had been dealing with and letting Him know how frustrated I was. God spoke and gave me half the answer to my frustration, and this is what I heard: "Parents are part of the problem."

Yes, you read that correctly. Parents are part of the problem. They are not the whole problem, but part of it. Let me stress that one more time before you throw this book across the room or just close it.

> *Parents are part of the problem. They are not the whole problem.*

I was frustrated because it seemed like we were having these great services every week, but had to come back the following week and start all over again. Week in and week out, we were dealing with the same issues. They seemed to experience God in a powerful way one

## PARENT'S INITIATIVE

week and come full circle by the next, as if nothing had occurred the previous week!

Don't get me wrong. Students must take responsibility for their part in this too. There are those situations in which parents are doing everything they can to no avail. I realize that students also have the responsibility to successfully walk out their relationship with God, but this process is also dependent on their parents and how they are walking out their relationships with God. In my thinking, it is really 50/50.

Parents play a bigger role than they want to take responsibility for. They are responsible for caring for their children's needs, preparing them as much as they can for life, shielding them from worldly influence, and helping them to become and leading them in becoming the man or woman of God they are called to be. Most importantly, they themselves are responsible for being the best example of Christ. As a student pastor, I find myself fighting battles with parents in equal measures to the ones I fight with students. This should not be.

Regarding those pictures, it is possible that the situation could not have been avoided. It would be wrong for me to sit here and say that it is a total reflection on bad parenting, because teenagers have a way of making stupid decisions on a daily basis.

For the sake of argument, let's just consider: What if the conversations we had had with the parents of this young lady were taken more seriously? What if they would also have noticed the compromise we saw in her life and held her more accountable? What if they had asked more questions about who she was hanging out with, where she was going, and even if other adults would be there?

I am not fifty by any means. I have not found one gray hair on my head to this day, nor do I have a lot of experience as a parent. My wife and I have only officially been parents for almost eight years. You may think that we do not have enough experience to be writing a book on parenting. However, my wife and I have been somewhat of a "father/mother" to many students for many years. I began when I turned

# THE PROBLEM

twenty, and my wife was just sixteen when she began ministering to young people.

Much has changed in student ministry, and a lot of it has not been for the best. It is getting harder to reach out to students effectively. It would help a lot if parents would do their part and have godly standards, not expect the church to raise their kids, and hold their kids accountable.

My wife and I have dealt with many parents, and we have seen the way they have raised their kids. We have seen some great parenting along with bad. Some parents are better than others in certain areas.

I am hoping we can learn together to be more aware of what is taking place in our homes, find out ways to possibly prevent some things from taking place, and work toward being the parents we are called to be. You may not know me, but believe me when I say that this is truly a God-given idea and not just another book on parenting. As I am writing this, I am sure that there will be times that I will be challenged to stop and reflect on some areas in my life and how I personally go about parenting. Things are constantly changing and evolving around us, but there are two things that always remain the same: God and His Word.

I never thought that I would write a book. If you were to ask my English teachers from high school if they thought I would write a book one day, they would have laughed. English was not my subject. I went to summer school prior to my senior year because I didn't want to take English 4 during my final year of high school. I wanted an easy A and crammed it all in.

I am not a writer by any means. At our church, we have everything proofread by other staff members, and they always make serious edits on my grammar. It has humbled me a lot to see all those marks on a manuscript I spent a lot of time on. So, I am not writing this because I am a great writer. I am writing this because this is what I know. I needed to write about this because we need to look at it together. When I woke up that Thursday morning and began to write, more and more came to me. It truly has been the Lord with me in all of this.

## PARENT'S INITIATIVE

Parenting is a journey. It never stops until the day you die. Over time, we all find ourselves helping to raise kids other than our own in some fashion. Whether we realize it or not, we do it. We do it at church, family gatherings, at the store, when we babysit for someone, and so on. Someone once said that it takes a village to raise a child. We are all a part of that village in some way or other.

When it comes to parenting, one of the best tools that many parents fail to utilize is the Bible. There are many stories and examples of some great (and bad) parenting in it. You can also find proverbs about how we should go about raising our children. There are stories that we can apply to situations in our homes and the methods we use in raising our children.

As you read this, it may seem that I am frustrated and just venting. If it comes across in that manner, I truly do apologize. I am just tired of seeing this generation of parents fail time and time again in their walk with God, especially when they can find more success with the help of better parenting and guidance. Many parents are committing a huge injustice against their own children.

God has placed our children in our hands for a reason. This responsibility has been taken lightly by many. I have often heard parents blame God for the way their children turned out, yet it could be due instead to the compromise in their personal lives. They just allowed the Enemy to have free rein and opened the door to their homes, saying to Satan, "Have your way. You can have me and my family. I am not willing to hold myself, or the children God has blessed me with, accountable."

As you read this, do me a huge favor and take your time. If you really like to read it could take you just one day, but don't let this just be another book that you read and put on your shelf to collect dust. Take it in slowly and work on some of the areas you may need to work on. Mark it up with a highlighter and refer to it later. Let it be a tool that helps you along the journey of being a parent and something to which you refer repeatedly.

# THE PROBLEM

We are in this together! You are not alone! Even though it may seem like it at times, you are not—God is at your side every step of the way. You may realize as you read that you have failed as a parent thus far, but I believe in a God who offers redemption. I believe in a God that offers forgiveness. I believe in a God who offers restoration. I believe in a God who offers grace and mercy. I believe in a God who promises to be with you in all things as an individual and even as a parent. I believe in a God who is not done with you yet, as long as you have a heartbeat and you are breathing. Let's take this journey together.

## Application Questions for Chapter 1

1. If you are a parent, do you agree that parents are part of the problem? If so, in what way(s)?
2. In what way(s) can it be frustrating for the local church when dealing with parents?
3. How are you partnering with ministry leaders in your church when it comes to your role as a parent?
4. ACTION STEP: Can you relate to how frustrating it was to see the pictures I described in this chapter? If this applied to your current situation with your own children, what did you change to prevent this in your own family?

## Chapter 2: First Things First

"The Lord makes firm the steps of the one who delights in him" (Psalm 37:23 NIV).

To become the parents God has called us to be, we must make sure that our relationship with Him is in order. Our lives need to be aligned with the path that He has set for us. We can't lead our families in the right direction if we are not following God as He directs.

For some time now, I have been on a journey that has truly drawn me closer to Jesus. I began to realize that my life was not all about me. It's really all about Him. As I began to get a grasp on this simple way of thinking, it began to change me. I began making sacrifices that I once thought impossible. I let go of things that were strongholds in my life. I found myself becoming a better person, a better husband, a better father, a better friend, and even a better minister to those around me. It wasn't like I had this horrible sin in my life that was causing this huge gap between me and God, either. There were simply some areas that I just never gave over to Him. As much as I hate to admit it, there was some compromise in my life.

I was living more for myself than for Him. I was watching what I wanted to watch and listening to what I wanted to hear without checking those areas with Him first. I was saying what I wanted to say, often not thinking twice about it. I was thinking what I wanted to think and not trying to decipher my thoughts. I was not submitting all of me to Him. More and more, I was doing things out of obligation rather than out of relationship. Because of that, it was easier for me to live for me and not for Him. I was riding the fence in how I lived my life. I was living for myself and no one else. You can't ride the fence and expect God to truly move in your life.

> "So humble yourselves before God. Resist the devil, and he will flee from you. Come close to God, and God will come close to you. Wash your hands, you sinners; purify your hearts, for your loyalty is divided between God and the world. Let there be tears for what you have done. Let there be sorrow and deep grief. Let there be sadness instead of laughter, and gloom instead of joy. Humble yourselves before the Lord, and he will lift you up in honor" (James 4:7–10).

Jesus wasn't the center of my life. Jesus wasn't my number one. I did pray on a daily basis, memorize Scriptures, and read my Bible daily, but it was because I knew I *had* to do that. I challenged others to do it, so it was only right for me to do it as well. I had it wrong for a long time too—even when I was involved in ministry. Looking back at my life, I can see how it happened. It was really easy to make it all about me and not Him, and it affected me in a great many ways. It affected my relationship with Him, my marriage, my family, my ministry, and my personal life.

When I began to focus my heart on Jesus again, I saw my life change. It was a process. It wasn't something that happened overnight. We often look for instant results, but we must be willing to work through the process. I became increasingly aware that something was wrong in my life. I became more aware of sin. As I became more aware of that sin, I began to sin less. Things that were important to me before became less important; I was becoming more like Him. I continue to work on this daily, and I know I will be for the rest of my life. That may sound discouraging, but it is not. I have a goal and a clean and joyful life.

## FIRST THINGS FIRST

"Because we have these promises, dear friends, let us cleanse ourselves from everything that can defile our body or spirit. And let us work toward complete holiness because we fear God" (2 Corinthians 7:1).

When your focus is Jesus and not yourself, you will reflect more on Him. This will affect you in more ways than you might think. You will sin less. You will find yourself working more towards holiness and living to the standards that He has set for you in His Word. You will make better decisions. You will draw closer to Him, and your life will just be better all around. Period. The question you need to ask yourself is whether He is truly first in your life. Is your life all about you and less about Him? This is a choice we all make. In the grand scheme of things, though, it really has been all about Him from the beginning.

"In the beginning the Word already existed. The Word was with God, and the Word was God" (John 1:1).

Right now, you can make that choice to put Him first and ask Him to forgive you for living your life for yourself, instead of Him; and for making it more about you and less about Him.

"If we confess our sins, he is faithful and just and will forgive us our sins and purify us from all unrighteousness" (1 John 1:9 NIV).

If you never made the choice to accept Him as your personal Lord and Savior, you can make that choice now. Or maybe you would like to rededicate your life to serving Him. You can do that as well.

"If you confess with your mouth that Jesus is Lord and believe in your heart that God raised Him from the dead, you will be saved. For it is by believing in your heart that you are made right with God, and it is by confessing with you moth that you are saved" (Romans 10:9–10).

## PARENT'S INITIATIVE

I have had the privilege and honor of leading many people to the Lord. There is a simple method I was taught that has helped me to lead people into making that decision. It is called the ABCs of salvation. This is how it goes:

1. **A**ccept that you are a sinner and that you need Jesus.

2. **B**elieve that Jesus died and rose from the dead for your sins.

3. **C**onfess Jesus Christ as your personal Lord and Savior.

I base this simple prayer off that. If you are ready to make that decision, whether it's for the first time or the third time doesn't really matter. It is not how many times you have said it that matters, it is that you decide in your mind that this is the final time you will need to say it. Pray this prayer:

> *Jesus, come into my life and change me. Forgive me for my sins and help me become who You want me to be. I believe that You died on the cross for my sins and rose from the dead. I need You and I confess with my mouth that You are my Lord and Savior. Amen.*

*What happens next is vital.* Tell someone about the decision you just made. Call, text, use social media, or even get in the car and go to a local church or family member or friend's house—someone you know who has a real relationship with God. Most people know of someone who is a real Christian. Get this person to get you headed in the right direction. If they are truly walking it out, then they will know what to do. If you don't know of someone like that, go to this website to get help with the next step and even provide you with more details about the decision you just made: www.followchrist.ag.org.

The key is to find a strong church, not just any church. You want a church that's a full-gospel church, one that has the evidence of the Spirit of God in it. A church is not there to make you feel good; a church should help you grow and lead you to be all that God has called you to be. It should have a strong children and student program, one where your

## FIRST THINGS FIRST

children can be involved and grow in their relationship with God too. You can tell when a church has a goal of having a strong family-oriented ministry because they invest heavily in ministries for the whole family.

There are churches out there that just want high attendance. They will do whatever they can to do it. They will water down the Word of God and tell you just enough to keep you coming. I am proud to be serving in a church that allows God to move and is faithful to what God says in His Word. I have personally grown because of that. It's not about you, it's about Him.

Once you find this church, get plugged in. Become a member and get involved in ministry. This is also vital because you are more than likely not going to grow spiritually if you are jumping from church to church. As you get involved in ministry, you will make strong connections in the church and will continue to get rooted and established.

Make church a PRIORITY in your home. More and more these days, families are going to church when it's convenient. I am glad that Jesus didn't die for me out of convenience. He did it because it was necessary. He did it because He first loved me. We also need to go to church because it is necessary. If you want your kids to continue to go to church when they get older, make church a priority now. Don't hop from church to church. Don't become one that doesn't get grounded and rooted. My pastor says that if you want to be fed, you must be willing to work (serve). One of the best ways to get fed in any church is to get involved. Ultimately, you are responsible for feeding yourself spiritually. You do that by praying, reading your Bible, and putting what you read in the Bible into action.

> "And let us not neglect our meeting together, as some people do, but encourage one another, especially now that the day of his return is drawing near" (Hebrews 10:25).

Why is all this in a book about parenting? Because for us to be successful parents, we must be following Jesus for real. It is ultimately all about Jesus. It's not about us. When we make it about Jesus, He

## PARENT'S INITIATIVE

changes everything. This decision changes the way we live our lives. It changes our priorities. It changes the way we entertain ourselves. It changes our attitude. It changes the way we make decisions. It changes the way we react. It changes the way we parent our children. Let me emphasize it again: It is Jesus that changes everything. When we allow Him to have complete access in our lives and continue to align ourselves to His plan and purpose for our lives, it makes life a lot easier and better.

An illustration was given on what it is like for God to live in a heart in which all those things are present. Let's just say that you go to a close friend's house and they ask you to come in, and proceed to give you a cup of coffee. Then they insist that you get comfortable and make yourself at home. All of sudden, your friend starts arguing with their spouse right in front of you. I don't know about you, but that would make anyone really uncomfortable. There may be some of you that would like to have a soda and a bag of popcorn, but it is one thing to watch a conflict in a movie and another in the home of a friend or family member.

If we want to be a comfortable "home" for the Spirit of the Lord, then we need to work on getting rid of the junk in our lives and in our homes. When it comes to the things that we have in the inner parts of us, we need to be engaged in things that please and honor Him. What comes out of our mouths should be pleasing to Jesus. Our desire should be that God can reside in us and truly be comfortable living in us. It's important that we take the time to reflect and take inventory of what goes on in our hearts and minds. When we stop and examine those things, it shows God that we are trying our best to provide a home that is comfortable and won't feel uneasy. We've got to do our best to make that possible on a daily basis.

The best example of Jesus that our children can see every day is us. As we take care of our "home," the actual place that we call home will be a place where God can also dwell. This is an area that I continue to work on, and I know I will for the rest of my life. We are all called to be like Christ. It's something that more and more Christians are taking lightly, and I don't want to be *that one* who does. Neither should you!

## FIRST THINGS FIRST

There are those who have become somewhat distant from God. I have noticed this through the way they are worshipping and engaging in church. Once they were in the front, truly worshipping their hearts out and really making an effort; but as time passed, they slowly fell back into the crowd and became distant. Some just stand there with a blank stare on their face, not engaging at all in worship. They are simply attending church.

The irony of it all is that when this happens, it stretches across the entire family! The parents distance themselves and disengage, which affects their kids. When parents are engaging and being involved, it will be easier for their kids as well. When parents are becoming more like Jesus, it will be easier for kids because they have an example to follow. Parents set the spiritual gauge in their homes. If Mom and Dad are hungry for more of God in their lives and on fire for God, then it will be easier for their kids to follow suit. I have a deep respect for those students with no godly examples in their homes who are still passionately pursuing God. It's sad that there are a lot of students who are on fire and hungry for the things of God and whose parents are not.

> "Those who say they live in God should live their lives as Jesus did" (1 John 2:6).

This is a goal toward which we should all strive. We will never arrive and be exactly like Him because of sin, but we should always continue to try our best. The key is that we are working toward it. As we draw close to Him, He will draw closer to us. To know Him requires for us to spend time with Him. This is a beautiful journey that will never end. We weren't meant to do this alone, but with others. If you would like to get a little more in-depth about who Jesus is, then read the books Matthew, Mark, Luke, and John: the four gospels found in the Bible.

Once again, it's not about you; it's all about Him. He changes everything! As you grow in Him and learn to be more like Him, you will be heading in the right direction. He will help you be the parent you are called to be and live the life He destined you to live.

# PARENT'S INITIATIVE

## Application Questions for Chapter 2

1. Have you accepted Jesus Christ as your personal Savior? Do you need to rededicate your life?
2. How is Jesus the center of your life?
3. How are you showing your children that He is the center of your life?
4. Are you involved in ministry at a local church? In what way?
5. ACTION STEP: If you have accepted Christ, tell someone!

# Chapter 3: Warning Label

"If you reject discipline, you only harm yourself; but
if you listen to correction, you grow in understanding"
(Proverbs 15:32).

There is a lot of humor to be found in warning labels. I was reading in my "office" the other day while I was taking care of some important matters. There are not many parents that are blessed enough to have an actual office in their homes, so they sometimes refer to their "office" as the bathroom. It's one of the few places where you can sneak away and get some privacy. When you have a small child in the house, the concept of going to the bathroom really doesn't resonate with them.

My daughter, if I let her, would hang out with me there and sit and watch me. As she grew older, she would bang on the door and almost cry because I would not let her in my "office." My son, on the other hand, left me alone in there when my daughter was younger. He was old enough to understand that this was not the place to "hang out" and watch their parent take care of some important "business."

A couple of years ago I came across a book at a yard sale. It was a great investment for our "office." It contained a lot of neat facts, and you could easily find yourself losing track of time while reading it. I came across a funny section about warning labels that can actually be found on some products with crazy things, such as telling the owner of a costume with a cape that it doesn't enable the user to fly, or instructing

## PARENT'S INITIATIVE

those using a collapsible stroller to remove the infant from the stroller before folding it up..

I have a warning label, too, for this book. This is my warning label:

WARNING: This book is just a tool. It was written to help you become more aware of what may be taking place in your home and offer possible improvements and changes you can make. It is not intended to give you instructions on being a parent. In no way am I implying that I have all the answers.

One more warning: If you have known me for some time, you may be an example in this book. I did not use real names, but can't promise that people will not connect the dots. I apologize and will be the first to admit that I am not perfect either, by any means.

Let me be honest. We all need help as parents. I sometimes find it difficult to take advice from other parents, especially when that advice makes me feel like one of those horrible parents. Sometimes people sort of tell you that in so many ways. There are times when either your own parents, family members, or close friends are breathing down your neck and constantly giving you advice. And then you get that friendly word from the random old lady at the store. You try to be nice (you don't want to be disrespectful), so you just smile and keep your mouth shut.

If you are like most parents, you don't like to be told that you are making mistakes as a parent. Most people do not like to be told what they are doing is wrong in any area! Face it! We're a proud bunch. I am guilty of being proud at times, and I am sure others will agree with that too. The mentality that we can do this on our own, and don't need any advice, is wrong.

We must learn to be open to others, trusting in God. God will use others to help us see situations of which we are unaware, or areas in which we fall short. Pride can blind us to problems that others can see clearly.

*Parent's Initiative* is not about telling parents how to raise their kids. It's about creating awareness in some areas that may have fallen through the cracks. To become aware of these areas is vital to our success as

## WARNING LABEL

parents. The next step lies in taking the initiative in making some improvements in those areas, especially when God has been dealing with you in these areas already and nothing has been done. The mission statement is as follows:

*Parent's Initiative* exists to create awareness in parents and provide them with tools that will help them become the parents God desires them to be.

Having initiative is taking action or having a game plan to take care of problems that you may be currently facing. It comes down to doing something about them and no longer waiting for them to somehow get better on their own.

This is not an answer to parenting. This is an act or strategy to help resolve some difficulty or to help your situation at home with your kids. I am hoping that this will help you become more aware and give you a fresh approach into becoming the parent that God intends you to be. If things are not going too well for you at home with your kids, then it might be time for a fresh approach. It may be time to make some necessary changes.

I know this much about parenting: It's not easy. Many of the problems that arise in our homes are problems that we may have had a hand in creating. As I mentioned earlier, kids are not the smartest ones on the block and they will make stupid decisions at times. We, as parents, can be just as guilty in making stupid decisions. Yet, there is always room for improvement.

I remember talking to a parent after another great service in our student ministry. This parent just recently had some serious problems with their child. It had to do with the Internet. This student was communicating with someone online and sharing details that they had no business sharing. I told the parent that I talked to their child, who was really broken from the whole situation. I talked to this parent for a few moments and this is how I finished the conversation:

*"There are so many parents that fail to realize that they*

## PARENT'S INITIATIVE

*have allowed the Enemy (Satan) free access to their homes. It's their responsibility to be careful what they allow to come in their homes. It's also their responsibility to protect their child and not allow free access to things that can harm them."*

I told her that she wasn't a horrible parent, and she began to cry. There are just some things that we cannot control. I could tell that she felt like she had made terrible mistakes as a parent. She was embarrassed, but now that she knew about it she also knew what to do from that moment on. It was her responsibility to do something about it. Action needed to be taken. She had to protect her home.

It would be absolutely foolish to have something like this take place and do nothing about it. Yet that happens all the time. I've heard it said: "To not make a decision is a decision, and to not take any action at all is taking action."

This parent could have decided to do nothing about this whole situation and simply watch the problem reoccur, which would have allowed more harm to come to her child. I am happy to report that this set of parents came to an agreement. They took the child's phone away and prevented unsupervised access to the Internet. It wasn't easy to take the phone away because of the lack of communication that it caused, but it was necessary. It wasn't easy to not allow access to the web because of schoolwork, but it was necessary. This parent became aware of a situation in her home and took the initiative. They came up with a strategy to resolve a difficult situation and their daughter got the picture. They had to step up to the plate, take responsibility, and help their daughter—and they did.

If you are looking for answers, you may not find it in this book. My number one goal is to give you some warning signs. I want you to be more aware of the dangers your children face than ever before. It's totally up to you to take the initiative once you become aware.

Parents, we have a responsibility; and it is time that we begin to take it more seriously. Being a parent is a call that God has placed on your

## WARNING LABEL

life. I continue to ask God in my prayers to help me be more patient and continue to push forward. I have dealt with a lot of "drama" while working with students that could have been avoided. Parents could have avoided many problems by nipping these things in the bud instead of letting them grow. Parents need to keep their children accountable and instill important values in them instead of relying on the church to do these things.

In some families, multiple people have come alongside the parents and invested energy and time in an effort to help them. There are people all around the parents trying their best to give solid advice, create more awareness, and offer parenting help, and the parents still choose to do what they want to do instead. I understand rejecting the advice of those offering help with wrong intentions, but more times than not the advice is being given out of a pure heart and good motives. The means of having awareness has been given, and these parents refuse to take it. Later, when a bad situation arises, they run to God, a pastor, or even a close friend for help. Sometimes we just want to say, "I told you so," but we refrain from saying those words. I know I hate hearing them myself. Nevertheless, the cycle continues.

I was reading Exodus 16 the other day, and I found myself encouraged from the perspective of being a minister. (Take a few moments and read Exodus 16.) This is what I got from it: No matter what you say or do, people will still do what they want to do. Some people just need to learn the hard way.

Parents have been given the "tools" to be a better parent, and yet we neglect them a lot of times. I want to encourage you to not neglect this tool that I feel God has given me. It's not just by chance that you find yourself reading this book. I believe it's God-appointed. You can be a great parent and your kids headed in the right direction, but if you are not careful and aware, things can change for the worse before you know it. Compromise can come in. If we neglect the principles we have worked so hard to instill, the tide can slowly turn and things can quickly go downhill.

## PARENT'S INITIATIVE

Please take the time to consider these words. Some of you may get defensive and say that what you are reading doesn't apply to you, when it really does. You might also find yourself saying, "I need to make sure so-and-so needs to read this," when it really was meant for you. Allow the Holy Spirit to speak to you and maybe even make you aware of some areas you may need to change. The warning signs are there in our lives. I am sure you will be able to at least take something from this book that will help you become a better parent. It is never too late to implement change. It's never too late to take the initiative and make some improvements. Whether your kids are still home or not, you can still make an impact.

> "Using a dull ax requires great strength, so sharpen the blade. That's the value of wisdom; it helps you succeed" (Ecclesiastes 10:10).

To take wisdom from others is to set ourselves up for success. It is crazy how we will neglect the wisdom we have around us and continue to expect things to improve. It's like chopping a tree down with a dull ax. That will require a great deal of strength and energy, but you will speed up the process if you ax is properly sharpened. To glean of others and even learn from the mistakes of others is only going to improve our lives.

When we first become parents, we don't really have a clue what to do. A lot of us thought that we could handle it, but let's be honest: it was overwhelming. You may have had some "skills" and even some "tools," but you still weren't truly prepared for all of it. At times you still may think: *What was I thinking, wanting to have kids?* Others truly enjoyed every minute of it, even the countless hours of nonstop going and the way the world seemed to revolve around your kids and their needs. There are many parents out there who, when it comes to parenting, have a "dull ax." They need to begin to sharpen it and take some action. Thankfully, there are many tools out there that will help you become a better parent. I hope this can be one of them.

# WARNING LABEL

On the morning that I woke up and began to write this, I felt the Lord break it down to me this way. At first it seemed that I was just writing out of frustration, but after about an hour it became more than that. I had a hard time stopping. It was like it was given to me, and put very simply. I am not a person of many words. My wife takes care of that department for me. She is the talker, and a lot of times I just sit back and let her do all the talking.

This is what I have done: I have taken letters from parents. I was given acronyms to go along with each letter. An acronym is a word formed by the initials of all its parts. (Between you and me, I had to look that up.)

My prayer is that God will reveal some things to you and give you the strength and patience to implement some changes, that He will help you to be more aware and also to take the initiative. You are not in this alone. Millions of other parents all around the world are struggling as well. This is not about me telling you how to be a parent or what you are doing wrong. We are in this together. We need to pray for one another, help one another to be more aware, and take action!

## Application Questions for Chapter 3

1. What warning labels fit your home?
2. How do you feel about being given advice on being a better parent from other people? Is this something you need to work on?
3. How do you go about getting more insight on your role as a parent? Is this something you can improve on?
4. ACTION STEP: The first "action" you can take feels like it is not an action at all, except for the fact that it requires carving out a little bit of time. Make a commitment to spend at least fifteen minutes each day praying: just talk to God about your life and your family. Tell Him about all your fears and frustrations. Pour out your heart. God is faithful. Not only will He meet with you, but He will begin to give you His solutions and answers as you walk through life as a result.

# Chapter 4: My Life, Family, and Parents

"The Lord is like a father to his children, tender and compassionate to those who fear him" (Psalm 103:13).

## My Life

I thought it best that you would get to know me a little more before we really get into the meat of why I felt I should write this book. If you are not interested in knowing my past and where I am today, then go ahead and go on to the next chapter. It will not bother me at all because I will not know. However, I hope that reading it will add to my credibility from other parents that have been raising little "mini-me" versions of yourself for some time now.

It's hard to read a book about parenting from someone with little real "experience" as a parent. Let's be honest. If you have been around church long enough, you know that your heart can turn away when you hear someone say that the Lord laid "this word on their heart." You have that response because you know that people use this as a cover for sharing their own advice. It is not a word from the Lord at all: it is a word from them. This practice has been abused and used to mislead a lot of people, so much so that it is an automatic turnoff for some; I hope that's not the case for you. There are still real words from God, and I believe that this book is one of them.

I was born in Philadelphia. When I was around four years old, we moved to a very small town called Interlachen, Florida. I really don't

## PARENT'S INITIATIVE

remember much about living in Philadelphia, but for some reason I remember when we moved from there. We moved from the city life to literally nothing but the woods. We lived in a double-wide trailer, and the roads leading to the main highway were dirt roads. In some areas, it was like quicksand. It was a dramatic experience for me, and it would be safe to say that it may been one of the best parenting decisions my parents ever made. There is no telling where I would be today if I had been raised in the city.

We didn't have much growing up, and that meant life would have been rough for us in Philadelphia. Looking back at those neighborhoods and the schools there, it was a miracle of sorts that we got out at all. Who knows if I would even be alive if I had been raised there. I may have ended up using or selling drugs or in a gang. Some of my extended family is still there and some of them are living a rough life. Yet there are those who are successful and have a strong family unit.

I was raised around the church. My dad became a pastor of a small church when I was around eight years old. For the most part, I was a "good" kid. I had my moments growing up, however, and when I was in middle school I made a choice that changed the direction of my life. I know that it may be hard to believe that a kid would make a decision like that at such a young age, but looking back, it was a huge decision and the first of many that impacted me for the good.

I was in the sixth grade and not doing well in school. My grades were poor, and I went to the dean's office quite a bit. My wake-up call came when I was sent to the dean's office and got a spanking from the dean himself, only to get another one when I got home. It wasn't the first or last time either. To get two or more spankings in one day during this time of my life was the norm.

But that day, I finally realized that I needed to make some changes. We lived in an area where there really wasn't much to do, and we all came from families that were just trying their hardest to make ends meet. When all those factors were mixed together, it usually led to a lot of trouble. My friends and I had very little to do and no money, which led to us being bored and finding trouble. Over time my friends were finding themselves going more in the wrong direction and making poor choices, and it led to some of them even getting arrested at times. I made the choice to hang out more with other people who were making good grades and staying out of trouble. This simple decision had major repercussions in my life.

When I was around thirteen, a prophetic word was spoken into my life. It was at a service at my dad's church that I was called into the ministry. A lot of my teenage years were spent "riding the fence" in my relationship with Christ. It would be safe to say that it was more along the lines of being on the wrong side. I didn't do drugs, I did drink a couple of times, and I did find myself "dating" a lot. There were those moments when I was on "fire" for God, but I always ended up putting the fire out by the choices I made. It really came down to compromise in my life. I had surrounded myself with the right people but still wanted to live my life on my terms, just like a lot of teenagers do.

Another turning point in my life was when my parents didn't make me attend their church but allowed me to attend another. I know that may seem kind of crazy; I am still shocked by it myself. Could you imagine being a pastor of a church and not making your own son attend it? I am sure that letting me to go to another church sent the wrong message to his congregation, but my father allowed it anyway. The only way I could have pulled it off was through God. It was another one of those turning points. All I know is that I probably wouldn't be where I am today if it weren't for that.

I will be forever grateful to my father for not allowing his pride to direct him and allowing me to attend another church. Looking at this today, it would be really difficult for me to allow my own son to attend another church. Why did he let me go? His church really didn't have a strong student ministry. In many ways, I was falling through the cracks. He saw that. I needed a change of scenery and someone who understood me. I wasn't handling the pressure of being the senior pastor's son very well either. Being in a small church like that only put the "magnifying glass" closer on me. It seemed like everyone was judging me and watching my every move. I had no room

## PARENT'S INITIATIVE

to make a mistake, and I felt trapped. My father saw all that and did the best thing for me, not the best thing for himself. It was an excellent parenting decision.

That other church that I started attending was right across from my high school. It was there that I truly began to get a concept of Jesus. I was under two great youth pastors who really invested in my life. One of them introduced me to a program that would play a huge role in my life. The director of this program met me at a student rally, talked to me afterwards, and was obedient to the Lord. He gave this on-the-fence poor kid a full scholarship to attend Master's Commission, a nine-month discipleship program.

It was one of those nights that I wasn't supposed to be there. Again, God's hand was upon me. Long story short: I was engaged to a girl that really didn't care much about God or the church. We were sexually active and in "love." Let's just say that I was a little confused and once again heading in the wrong direction. I was supposed to hang out with her that night, but I chose to go to church anyway because the current youth pastor had really urged me not to miss that particular service.

It's crazy when you really think about it. God truly had His hand on my life. Everything lined up to this point. He had a purpose specifically for me, and a lot of it came about by me just slightly listening to Him and Him placing the right people in my life along the way. What if I would have chosen otherwise in just one area? What if I had not left my fiancée's apartment on that Wednesday afternoon and hung out with her that evening instead? There are so many variables and what ifs. There are many life stories full of "what ifs," and mine is definitely one.

I went to Master's Commission in Decatur, Alabama; and while I was there, God really got ahold of me. I needed to get away from what I knew and what I was comfortable with. God opened this door for me to capture my heart. I got the opportunity to travel all over the United States, doing school assemblies, church services, rallies, and seeing hundreds (if not thousands) come to know Jesus as their personal Lord

## MY LIFE, FAMILY, AND PARENTS

and Savior. It truly propelled and prepared me to be who I am today and directed me in my personal relationship with God as well.

### My Family

I met my beautiful wife at the beginning of my second year of Master's Commission. We got married eleven months later. Only God could have worked that out. My wife knew she was going to spend the rest of her life with me the moment we met. She actually saw my picture before she met me and knew that I was the one. I guess she couldn't resist my infectious smile.

It took more time for me, of course. It was a month and half after we met that I knew. We were at a retreat in Springville, Alabama, overlooking a lake. It was a beautiful day. We had a few moments alone, just talking. Finally, I had the guts to ask her: "How do you know that you want to spend the rest of your life with me?" The answer I got was confirmation and straightforward.

This is how she put it. There was no denying she knew what she wanted. She said she wanted to spend the rest of her life with me. She wanted to have my babies and grow old with me. (She had me when she said that she wanted to have my babies.) Just kidding! It was just the way she said it that confirmed it. She said it with a confidence that I had only heard a couple of times at that point in my life. It was like she knew beyond a shadow of a doubt that it was God that brought us together.

We got married; and to be honest, the first couple of years were rough. You were probably expecting me to say that it was awesome. The truth is that when you have personalities like ours, it could get a little crazy. Obviously, we worked things out. The thought of giving up never crossed my mind. I am sure the thought of killing me has crossed her mind, at least a couple of times. We have now been married for over fifteen years, and I am proud to say that my wife is not only my wife, but my best friend too.

# PARENT'S INITIATIVE

This book is not about marriage, but I do have this to say: Marriage is not something you can master, but it is something that you must continue to work on. We still have those rough days, but they are honestly few and far between. As we have drawn closer to God, we have learned to love, honor, and respect one another. We have two great kids, a son named Zane and a daughter named Marsaylah.

We truly enjoy parenting. (I am sure you expected me to say that.) I would be a liar if I did not tell you that it does have its days too. I am sure that many of you will agree. There are those times when you would like to take that child to the customer service desk and ask for a refund or an exchange. We pray every day that God will help us in our role as parents. My wife and I will be the first to tell you that we have made our mistakes and learned some things the hard way.

Thus far, I would like to think that we have done a good job of raising our kids. They are very appreciative and respectful. Those who have watched our kids have always had good things to say about them. Either our kids are really nice or they are just great liars. There have been times when people have complimented us on how good a job we are doing. It is great to hear that, and it reassures us that we are likely doing the right thing. Obviously, we are still in the process of raising our kids and will continue to do so. We will do it with God's help and direction.

We are increasingly disturbed because of the way events and cultural trends are unfolding around us though. Parenting is not becoming easier; it's getting much harder because of the direction this world is going in and the choices parents are making as they raise their children within and without the church.

## Something to Think About

My wife and I have been doing ministry together full time for over fifteen years. We truly love what we do and look forward to what each day holds. We find ourselves praying harder than even before and drawing closer to God. Since our culture is going downhill at such a rapid rate, though, it's getting harder to reach students. We have

# MY LIFE, FAMILY, AND PARENTS

noticed this over time, and I am sure you have as well. There is a great deal of compromise around us. What was unacceptable at one time is now acceptable. Areas in which people used to take a stand have shifted, and today they no longer take that same stand.

I look back and remember when I was a teenager in high school. There have been major changes from the way students carry themselves; how they respect one another; how they dress; their morals, attitudes, and priorities; and much more. I am sure that a lot of what's going on now was going on when I was a teenager, but it was behind "closed doors" then. Now it is out in the open.

When I was younger, there was a huge battle being fought for students by their parents. When students finally got ahold of it, they joined in the fight. Now the battle is being fought for students *and for their parents*. Many parents out there have allowed a lot of compromise in their homes. They are more concerned with being a friend instead of a parent to their child.

When I was growing up, it seemed like parents were more concerned for their kids and didn't back down. The parents that I was around in the church growing up seemed to be stronger spiritually and held their children to a higher standard. In many ways today, that seems to be more relaxed. Don't get me wrong; there are some parents out there who are fighting hard for their children, but overall that seems less prevalent in the parents I see as a whole.

## My Parents

Both of my parents came from broken homes. My dad didn't know his father, and my mom didn't know hers. They had it really rough growing up. To not have a father present in anyone's life can be difficult. I know it was hard for my parents because they never really talked about it. It would be safe to say that I never heard my dad say anything about his father. My mom thought that she met her dad on one occasion, but really wasn't sure.

## PARENT'S INITIATIVE

I cannot imagine what it would be like to be raised without a father. My mom married my dad at a young age. My dad had been recently divorced. My mom didn't have the blessing of her mother, and that made it a little rough for them from the beginning. To say that my parents had a good example of what it would take to be great parents would be a stretch. It was a different time and, in some ways, a cultural thing. There is no doubt in my mind they did the best they could with the means they had.

I don't want to seem ungrateful for my parents in any way, so this is the hardest part of my story to write about. I love my parents deeply, and I know they sacrificed a lot over the years that I lived under their roof. They went without many times so that my sister and I could have things we wanted. We didn't have much, but I know my parents worked hard. I cannot begin to tell you how many times over the last few years that my mom has told me she was sorry she was so hard on me. I continue to tell her that I am who I am today because she was. Because of their upbringing and what they faced during that time, my parents did well in raising my sister and me.

I was closer to my mom growing up because it was easier to be around her. It wasn't that it wasn't easy to be around my dad; it just seemed easier to approach my mom. I know my dad loved me, but we really didn't talk much. It would be safe to say that the reason my father was so quiet was because he didn't really have a father in his life. Yet I knew growing up that he loved us deeply.

I will never forget the day my dad took me fishing; it was probably the most memorable day that I had with him. To this day, when it comes up, he denies that I caught more fish than him. I will also never forget the day he told me that he was proud of me and loved me after my high school graduation ceremony. It was the way that he said it that night. He had told me the same thing on several different occasions, but it just came out differently that night. I will never forget it.

My parents are divorced now. It breaks my heart to say that because it seemed that they would be together the rest of their lives. I love both of them a lot, and I owe a lot to them. They sacrificed themselves

## MY LIFE, FAMILY, AND PARENTS

for me. They expected a lot out of me and always pushed me to do my best in school. They made sure that I never did without, but they didn't spoil me.

When I turned sixteen, my mom actually went out and found me a job at a pizza place. From the moment I got my first paycheck, I was taught to manage my money. I paid for practically everything that I needed and when I found myself in a rough spot, my parents helped me out. If it weren't for that, I would have probably been in a bad place financially when I moved out. Would I trade them for another set of parents? No. Did I learn what to do and not do as a parent from them? Yes, the good and the bad.

I am sure that if my parents could go back and do some things differently, they would. Who in their right mind wouldn't if given the chance? We all have those things we wish we could take back. We all have those times we wish we could forget. There are those few moments that will forever be engraved in your mind. There are also those times as a parent that you find yourself doing some of the same things your parents did—the very things that you told yourself that you wouldn't do when you became a parent.

We have a responsibility to take all of our life experiences and do something with them. There is a reason we faced all the things that we have faced up to this point. We are to take the good and the bad and apply what we have learned to the way we raise our kids. Some had it really bad growing up and need to start completely fresh. But the majority can find a lot of great things they can take from their upbringing and apply it to the way they are raising their kids now. The key is that you raise them the way God intended. To do this requires that you are spending time in prayer and in the Word. When it comes to parenting, or any area of our personal lives, we can't neglect our past experiences. We can learn a lot from them as we continue to move forward.

# PARENT'S INITIATIVE

## Application Questions for Chapter 4

1. How was your childhood experience with your parents? How did they affect you? Has your experience affected the way you parent? In what ways?

2. If your childhood experience wasn't the greatest, do you find yourself doing some of the same things your parents were doing?

3. What are some positive experiences you had with your parents? How are you applying them now in your role as a parent?

4. What are some great memories that you have with your parents? Have you found ways to implement them now?

5. ACTION STEP: What would you have done differently during your childhood if you were the parent (of you)? Are you applying those ideas now? How could you apply them now?

# Chapter 5: Parenting Today

> "No, dear brothers and sisters, I have not achieved it, but I focus on this one thing: Forgetting the past and looking forward to what lies ahead, I press on" (Philippians 3:13–14).

When it comes to sin, past failures, past mistakes, even condemnation, I often find myself saying that we shouldn't live in the past. When we ask God for forgiveness for the sins we have committed, it is forever forgotten. Just as He has forgiven us, we should also forgive ourselves. There's a saying: "Yesterday is gone, today is a present, and tomorrow is mystery." Yesterday is forgotten, but today is a gift. What we do today is what really matters.

We tend to live too much in the past and hold on to it in an unhealthy manner. It's important that we ask God for forgiveness and move forward. When we hold on and don't move forward, it really affects our relationship with God. He has offered us forgiveness so we can move forward in Him. Our worst enemy really isn't Satan; many times, it's us. We tend to blame Satan for situations that he did not do. Very often, we are the ones who put ourselves in the situations we are in.

We need to learn from our mistakes. We are going to make mistakes every day. It's a given. We must learn from them and do our best to avoid them. In life we will fall (make mistakes); the key thing is that we pick ourselves up (understand why we fell), clean ourselves off (make it right), and continue moving forward (learn from it and do what we can to not make that mistake again). I say all that for a couple of reasons:

## PARENT'S INITIATIVE

1. Since we will make mistakes, we need to learn from them and grow. The key is to ask God for forgiveness and move forward. None of us are perfect. God wants us to grow. He understands us better than anyone else.
2. The same principle applies to parenting. We will make mistakes and must learn from them.

Don't have the mindset that there is no possible way you could make a mistake as a parent. The worst mindset that any individual could ever have is thinking they know it all. Someone like that will not listen to others or learn from their mistakes. When that mentality is present, pride is an issue. Pride always bears bad fruit.

There is much we can learn by listening to the parents of the past and seeing what was done well. A long time ago, our forefathers ran this country and did a pretty good job of it. Similarly, there have been good parents who have written about their experiences. I obviously didn't live in the 1700s or even the early 1900s! I was born in 1980. For me to say that "I remember when" would not be of value, because I do not. I only remember how things were better then, but it was beginning to take a turn for the worse as I got older. But there is a wealth of writings from the generations before us.

I once came across this interesting blog about "parenting today versus parenting yesterday." It really made me think about how things have changed. It hit me: We are living at a time that has so much information at our disposal. Just by doing a search on the Internet, you can have easy access to free counseling. You can read an article or watch a video that covers what you are currently dealing with. Obviously, you have to be careful who you take advice from and be sure to diligently research these individuals, but the information is there. We have all these resources available to us, and we should take advantage of it. We can truly learn a lot from parents of the past.

It would be safe to say that there have always been those kids who were considered "bad." There were those kids who waited for the moment their parents turned their heads so they could act like a fool,

## PARENTING TODAY

but it wasn't as often. Kids were more apt to show proper respect for those who were older than they were. In some ways, they were also less selfish. They knew how to work and were expected to do their part in their families.

We are now living in a time when kids are not as respectful and tend to be very rude. They also have a sense of entitlement and are often emotionally high-strung. Is this only because of the change of the times we are living in? Or would it be safe to say that parents are not being as diligent as they once were?

I think it's the latter. It seems that many parents have become lazier and would rather not deal with the obvious problems their kids have. Things haven't got better; they are only getting worse. The fact that it is harder to raise kids in this day and age should cause parents to fight even harder for their kids. Instead, parents are checking out. It is an inconvenience to even fight. This should not be.

At one time, there was a strong focus to make sure that children were trained in a good work ethic, respect, manners, being courteous, and being responsible. These values were instilled in children. It was work, and it required daily consistent attention. It was even a burden at times, but parents made the effort because they realized the importance of this training. The other factor that played a role was the access that children had to older generations. It was common for them to be raised around grandparents who helped teach these core values as well. It was important for everyone to have a role. It was a priority! Now it is left up to someone else to instill these valuable character traits in our children. Who? Teachers in schools, church leaders, and others: but these are not the people God put in place to pour into children. God created families. He gave children to parents so they could raise their children.

We live in an age of parenting extremes. There are parents who have abdicated their position, and there are those who are overly aggressive about it and never let their kids alone for a minute.

Even the level of our expectations has changed. Some parents are apt to hold their kid's hands every single step of the way. Back in the

## PARENT'S INITIATIVE

day, parents let go and stood at a close distance. They could see their kids learn things on their own, but could also be there when they were really needed. Today, some parents worriedly lead them every single second and do not let them learn on their own (or, as some would say, learn the hard way.) In earlier generations, the expectation for kids wasn't to walk this fine line of perfection but to learn and grow from their mistakes. There was this room allowed to make mistakes; and when a mistake was made, there were consequences. Discipline was a consequence. Explanation accompanied that discipline, along with directions about what not to do next time. There was an emphasis on a lesson being learned.

### Using the Yesterday Parenting Method

We dealt with a situation in our home recently in which we applied the "back in the day" method. My son Zane was fixing to wrap up another year at elementary school. One of the things that I love about this school is that they send daily reports along with the student. They put it in a folder along with any other handouts, homework, or important information.

We get an update on his behavior for the day and we sign the folder every day to verify we looked over it. (I am glad that we didn't get those when I was in elementary school. I would have gotten in a lot of trouble.) Back then, though, we did not really "need" those daily reports. The schools handled it differently, by either disciplining you or sending you to detention. Then you would go home and, possibly, get disciplined again. For some it would be another spanking to go along with what you got at school that day. You may even have been grounded on top of it all. It wasn't enough for some parents if their kids got it in school; they "spread the love." In society then, it was an embarrassment if your kids were not well behaved in school. Today, some people do not care.

Thus far I am proud to say that my son has only gotten in trouble in school a couple of times. Each time it has been for talking too much in class. (He gets that from his mother.) In kindergarten it was a little different. The teacher that Zane had was great, but we really felt sorry for her. This was her last year at the school because she was going to retire. I am not sure why they did this, but it seemed like she got the "perfect class" to retire with a bang. She had a lot of foreign students, some who could hardly speak English, and some students that seriously needed to be medicated. I don't really believe in medication, but these kids really needed it. I ate lunch with Zane a couple of times and helped at a couple of events. I would have done more, but I couldn't handle it. Needless to say, I had serious respect for this lady.

After the first day of kindergarten, Zane came home with this folder with a smiley face on it, and I thought that was cool. I thought it was a privilege and an honor to know how he was doing at school on a daily basis. That way if a problem arose, we could deal with it. I am sure he didn't get ahold of that concept because he thought it was pretty cool himself. A couple of days went by with more smiley faces ... and then the dreaded sad face came in the folder. When I picked him up that day, you could see something was wrong. He is usually happy and moving nonstop. I knew something was up. (If Zane isn't all peppy and wired, there is something going on. It's hard for him to hide it.)

He got in the car and told me that he got a sad face. It was for talking. He began to explain why, but I honestly wasn't listening to him closely because I believed the teacher's note more than his explanation. We took care of it.

A week or so went by, and he got another. Again, it was for talking. Again, we took care of it. In a week, he got yet another for the same thing, and we took care of it again. At this point I began listening more to Zane because I knew something was going on. Zane is definitely not some perfect kid, but it was unusual that he was not "catching on" by now. Usually after disciplining him a couple of times on something, he understands it and changes.

My wife wrote a letter to the teacher and asked her about it. She put it in the folder to be taken to school. The letter was very positive toward the teacher. We truly wanted to get to the bottom of it and in a way that would teach our son to respect his teacher. This letter was not to blast

# PARENT'S INITIATIVE

this teacher in any way. In it, my wife explained that we disciplined Zane and wanted further information about what was happening. Zane had been telling us that he wasn't talking when he shouldn't. He said he was actually listening. My wife emphasized that we wanted to help her in any way we could but needed more information about our son's behavior.

She wrote back saying Zane was a great student—and that at the end of the day when she was getting the folders ready, she really wasn't thinking: she was putting sad faces on *everyone's* folder. She wasn't aware that we were actually disciplining our son. Her class was a real handful. (Truthfully, if I had been teaching some of those students, I would put a huge sad face on every progress report too.)

The rest of that year, Zane didn't get another sad face. He behaved well, and I am almost certain that he did talk when he shouldn't have sometimes. Yet after a couple times of being disciplined, he knew that he needed to stop talking when it was not the right time for that.

Looking back at this situation, I am sure that there are some parents who would have gotten mad and stormed the school's front office to talk to the principal. I honestly wasn't upset about the situation. What bothered me more than anything else was continually receiving those sad faces home on a piece of paper with nothing being done about it. I am sure some parents just looked at it and didn't think twice about it. I am sure some of those parents looked forward to dropping their kids off and not having to worry about them for eight hours. They were relieved. They looked forward to the break. I am sure that teacher received some letters or phone calls about the way she taught and hardly ever got a letter or phone call from parents asking how they could help their child do better.

A lot of these parents allowed this behavior to continue with no discipline. They may have thought, *Kids will be kids*. They couldn't care less if someone else had to deal with their kids. Yet this is the best time to institute some structure and discipline. The only discipline some of these kids received was in school, and today you can only go so far with that. If the only discipline some of these kids ever got was a sad

# PARENTING TODAY

face on a piece of paper, God help us all. It's not going to get any better at that rate.

This is the direction that parenting is heading today, and it truly breaks my heart. To see how some parents handle situations today is scary. From how their kids handle conflict with other kids to how the parents handle their children's grades and behavior to the strange sense of entitlement present in youth, we are definitely not going in a good direction. Kids think they do not have to fight or work for what they have, and parents are fighting their kid's battles—even while they are in college. There are parents out there who are actually calling college professors and chewing them out on behalf of their young adult children. I am sure you can easily create your own list of the parenting changes you see today.

## Something to Think About

> "Such things were written in the Scriptures long ago to teach us. And the Scriptures give us hope and encouragement as we wait patiently for God's promises to be fulfilled" (Romans 15:4).

When it comes to parenting, past and present, our best source is the Bible. The Scriptures give us hope and inspire us to live the very things we read. We can easily reflect on our lives and the lives of others, seeing how His promises were fulfilled time and time again.

I once read an article about parenting that mentioned that the Bible says a lot about parenting, but you will only find a few specific instructions on how to actually parent. Those few specific instructions are all we really need. The fact is that doing everything we know how to do still doesn't guarantee that our kids will go in the right direction. In the end, they still have to make the right choice; they still have to decide whether they want to walk out their relationship with God.

Even God didn't have perfect kids! Adam and Eve chose to sin, but God handled their mistake the way a perfect parent would. (To say that

## PARENT'S INITIATIVE

God was not a perfect parent would be foolish.) We are the ones who are not perfect, just like Adam and Eve. They were His children, and so are we.

At the end of the day, it really boils down to us walking out our relationship with Him and trusting in Him. As we walk in Him, following Him on a daily basis, we will, in turn, submit everything and leave it all in His hands. The end goal is to implement what we find and read in the Word in our daily lives. As we do this, we realize that we're not the focus of the universe; then, we take action as parents that will guarantee this same outcome for our children. We need to do everything we can to be the parents that He has called us to be. We want them to come to the same realization that we did and be able to replicate the same kind of relationship with God that we ourselves have.

> "Blessed are those who listen to me, watching daily at my doors, waiting at my doorway" (Proverbs 8:34 NIV).

As we spend time in prayer and apply what we read in the Word, we will be blessed as parents. Those are two primary ways in which we listen and receive the blessing that God has for us. There was a mom that asked another mom, "How do you know if you're a good mom?" The response was simple: "I know I'm a good mom when I'm first a good daughter"; that is, being a good daughter to her true Father.

As we begin to break down the word *parents*, remember that our focus is on creating an awareness, and then taking the *initiative* once you have done that. You cannot make improvements until you are aware of situations that require change. This is not about a perfect solution, but emphasizing what is found in Scripture.

Some of you may already have implemented some of the things that you are about to read. Others, though, may be at a breaking point with a huge hill to climb. And then there are those who are simply trying to get a head start. That is great.

The key is to take one step at a time and trust God in each step you take. Be sure to continue working on yourself and your relationship with

## PARENTING TODAY

God. The fruit of that process will spread into other areas of your life. Parenting never stops, and adjustments always have to be made. If you have more than one child, you will quickly note that each one is unique, so your parenting may have to be done differently with each one. The principles are the same for all, but the approaches may be different. We are in this together. You are not alone!

### Application Questions for Chapter 5

1. From your perspective, what is right or wrong with parenting today?
2. Reflecting on the past, what are some things that you could implement more? How could you go about doing that?
3. Do you refer to the Bible at all when it comes to your role as a parent? If not, would you make a commitment to study more about it now?
4. ACTION STEP: What steps are you taking to learn from the mistakes you have made thus far as a parent? Sometimes it helps to get your ideas on paper. Do that today. As you look at your list, formulate a plan to make the changes you need.

# Chapter 6: Being Too Passive

> "About that time David's son Adonijah ... began boasting, 'I will make myself king.' So he ... recruited fifty men to run in front of him. Now his father, King David, had never disciplined him at any time, even by asking, 'Why are you doing that?' Adonijah had been born next after Absalom, and he was very handsome"
> (1 Kings 1:5–6).

Finding a balance in parenting is one of the hardest things to do. I often find myself struggling with this because I don't want to be too overbearing, nor do I want to be too relaxed about certain things. Not only do I want to find a good balance, I also want to be consistent. Consistency is vital in parenting. If there is no consistency in your home, good luck.

Even now, as young as my kids are, we see the need for both these things. We must have a solid foundation and know where we stand and what we expect. As our children get older, they will find themselves respecting that balance and consistency more. We are better off establishing it now rather than trying to build it later when it will not be as powerful in their lives. There is enough inconsistency and chaos going on in the world around them. We, as parents, should supply them with the balance and consistency in our homes that will give them a firm place to stand.

## PARENT'S INITIATIVE

Growing up, I saw both extremes. There were parents who were too passive and allowed anything and everything in their homes. Their kids had free rein. You could easily tell by the way they carried themselves and treated others. Passive parenting produced a lot of drama.

Then you had those parents who were borderline crazy and so aggressive that even though they disciplined their kids, it still turned out badly. Their kids had no room for error and were under constant watch. Every mistake was magnified and dealt with harshly. When they finally had a taste of freedom, because they were old enough to move out or they had "earned" it, they were like caged animals finally set free. They may have been a little timid at first, but in time, they rebelled. Their parents had failed to get ahold of their hearts, and it turned out being really bad for them.

Today, I see that even more. That's why I believe finding a healthy balance is so important. In the long run, if a balance is not found, it will bring problems. Let's be honest. Life is full of problems no matter what, but a balance lessens them. There will be less heartache, less drama, fewer sleepless nights, and even fewer mistakes because problems in the home are being dealt with the way they should be. Your kids will be well-adjusted and accustomed to what is expected from them.

Some parents have found some balance, and it's working for them. The key is to be aware of any areas in which you are too passive or too aggressive. We will be covering these in the next two chapters.

The sad truth is that the majority of parents are aware of problems in their homes yet are not doing anything about them. They are very aware of the potential for some pretty serious issues in their kids, but they either just don't want to deal with them or don't know how. They just let it go on, and it becomes a cancer that spreads. It spreads through the home and to other family members. Before they know it, it brings division and a lot of needless conflict!

God may even step in. He may intervene and make the parents even more aware, and still nothing is done about it. God will continue to put

## BEING TOO PASSIVE

forth His hand, making the parents aware through other individuals, situations, a sermon, or—as in my case—a direct word. (I was part of the problem.) But the parents must respond.

Being passive is the root of a multitude of evils. The majority of parents are aware of problems in their homes and in the lives of their kids, but are either afraid to address them or just too tired to fight anymore. They have given up hope and consider trying to make things better a pointless exercise that will only bring more drama and instability. Instead, they sit and count down the days till their kids will be out of the house, if that day ever comes.

Being passive is accepting things as they are. Passive people allow or accept things that happen without response or resistance. It's like getting hit with a ball in the face over and over again and doing nothing about it. You have this massive headache because of it, but you refuse to deal with it.

Being too passive as a parent is the worst thing we can do. A lot of the ideas in this book stem from dealing with out of touch or fearful parents who are too passive. They have either become too comfortable and lazy, or a lot of compromise can be found in their own lives. In the midst of that compromise they are blinded and have become passive in their responses to clear dangers, not only in their own lives but also in their homes. In this lack of action, free rein is given to the Enemy.

A lot of parents just sit back and accept their situation. Some of them allow the world to parent their kids by default, since they themselves are not doing it. Most are not as active in parenting as they should be, not responding as they should, or fighting back as they should. It's like they brought their kids into this world and then left them to fend for themselves. They set them up for failure. As their kids grow older, they wonder what happened to their babies. How did they drop the ball?

They begin to ask themselves these questions or even discuss them with their spouse: Why are the kids so disrespectful? Why is my daughter pregnant? Why don't they want to go to church anymore?

# PARENT'S INITIATIVE

How did it get to the point where my child is struggling with pornography? This questioning goes on and on in their minds. Why? How? When? Where? What? It began with being too passive and not taking responsibility from the very beginning. They never took the initiative to make the situation better.

I want to highlight some areas in which many parents are being too passive. You may think of other areas, but these are the ones I have noticed most. If you are like me, you may have glanced at the contents of this book. If you do, you will notice that some areas have been given special attention. These areas come up in this passive parenting category as well. A lot of bad parenting comes from being too passive and not dealing with things as we become aware of them. Compromise only paves the way for more problems in the future.

## Church

I spent a lot of time in church growing up. People like to complain about how often their church meets and how long their services are. I think I might have you beat in that department as a young child. I went to church twice on Sundays; these services lasted about two hours at the least. Monday night was for prayer, which meant we went to someone else's house and prayed for at least an hour. Wednesday night was Bible study night, and that took at least an hour and a half. Friday night was our last service for the week, and it took about two hours. Our family hardly ever missed a service. If we missed, it was because one of us was sick or we were on vacation.

Church was a priority, and we were there every time the doors opened. This consistent commitment and the fact that Jesus became real in my life are the main reasons I am in church today. It was instilled in me as a young child that church was a priority. When I turned sixteen, my parents gave me the choice to go to church or not. I began attending another church. There I was with the option to sleep in on Sunday mornings, but I didn't. Instead I found myself going to church. I could have worked on Wednesday nights, but I personally asked for them off so that I could attend church. Because

## BEING TOO PASSIVE

my parents made church a priority at home, I made it a priority in my life too. It was second nature to me, and I felt like something was missing if I didn't attend church on a consistent basis. The church that I attended didn't meet as often as my parents' church did, but I was there every Wednesday night and Sunday morning.

Parents have become way too passive when it comes to church. Church has become an afterthought. Some parents allow their children to miss it because they don't feel like going. Some allow their kids to miss it because they didn't manage their time wisely and decided to do a project for school at the last minute instead. They do this even after knowing when an assignment was due a couple of weeks in advance!

There is a private Christian school in our area that does not hand out homework on Wednesday nights. We had students not attend because they had procrastinated on other homework, so even though the faculty were doing their best to encourage going to the Wednesday night meeting, the parents still let their kids stay home. Instead of letting the student learn a valuable lesson about procrastinating on assignments, these parents justified missing church and let them catch up then. These students will never learn to plan their projects and take responsibility in such an atmosphere. The result is that these students think it's okay to wait to the last minute on anything they have been assigned. Similarly, missing church is also okay; it's really not that big of a deal. If I procrastinated as a child, I suffered the consequences and learned a valuable lesson.

The sad thing is that there are also students who miss church because their parents are too tired and don't feel like driving them. Interestingly, these same parents will do whatever they can to get rid of their kids other times, driving them all over the place, tired or not. That tired parent is allowing their child to miss an opportunity for God to do something in their life.

Other parents let their children miss church to play sports. I guess they are afraid that if little Johnny misses a practice, he will miss an opportunity for the majors at a young age. Reality is that there are

## PARENT'S INITIATIVE

very few, if any, professional or college recruiters lining up at Little League games across America with notepads and stopwatches. For some parents, it begins at the ripe old age of four and five with T-ball.

I am in no way implying that you will miss heaven by missing a service here and there, especially when there's a legitimate reason. The issue is when it's a regular occurrence, and missing church just happens. It really bothers me that attending church has become an elective in many of our lives. It's no longer regarded as a big deal if it's missed. When other events besides church are missed there's great regret, and more of an effort and sacrifice is made for these other events.

Culture has changed. This dramatic cultural change has changed the way we do ministry. Christian adults today have different views and values than those who have gone before them.

Think about it. There was a time when church was really important to more families than it is now. It may not have been as important for the children in the home, but it was extremely important for the parents. Many kids were forced to attend their student ministries; now, it seems, more often than not students are given the option of attending.

Church has been relegated to the bottom of the pecking order, either unintentionally or on purpose, because of the inconvenience. It goes like this: There are projects to work on or finish, other homework to complete, tests to study for, lack of rest, practices, sports, vacations, and —— (just fill in the blank). As long as these things are not going on, we will make to church. But those things will come first! Church is dead last in the pecking order of priorities.

For some parents, the idea of church as an "elective" doesn't affect them. Some parents have had a life-changing experience with God, and that experience has sustained them for a long time. It may last for the rest of their lives. I will never forget an experience I had on Aug. 11, 1999, in Orlando, Florida, during a youth conference. I still refer back to that moment in my life, and it serves as a reminder that

## BEING TOO PASSIVE

keeps me focused. It was a transformational and defining moment. The sad thing is that some parents may think that "their moment" with God should be sufficient for their children too. It never works like that, though. Our kids need to have their own moment with God. If church is an elective, then it's very possible that children will miss their moment or even many moments.

The church should be a priority in the home, especially when you are able to see the impact that it had on your life. Attending church should be something that you look forward to—not only for you, but also for your family. As much as our family is at the church, we all look forward to our "Family Night" service on Wednesday night and our Sunday morning services. When you think about the time that we actually spend in these services, it pales in comparison to all the time we spend doing other things. It is not that much time, but it is a huge investment.

It may be hard to get your kids to want to go to church, but it becomes easier as they get involved and make friends. It will be hard for them to do those things if they are rarely attending. Most of us thrive on building friendships and making connections; it's even more important for your children. Memories and lifelong friendships will be created as they become more involved and connected. If church is merely one more thing they do, it will be hard to establish those friendships.

It is ultimately up to parents to model a church commitment and not make going to church seem like a burden or just another event in your busy lives. Yes, this totally goes against what a lot of people believe. There are a lot of so-called Christians who have pushed their morals, priorities, and standards to the side and only practice and do the right things when it's convenient. The truth is that you need the church and the church needs you. Your family needs the church and the church needs your family. Together we develop one another and grow stronger.

# PARENT'S INITIATIVE

"And let us not neglect our meeting together, as some people do, but encourage one another, especially now that the day of His return in drawing near" (Hebrews 10:25).

## Something to Think About

This is something my pastor has said on several occasions. Why is it that a majority of parents don't give their kids the option of going to school, but when it comes to church the option is there? Why is missing work or even being late to work not an option, but missing church is? How is it that a majority of families that had kids involved in sports will do everything they can to be on time for a sporting event at 8 a.m. on a Saturday morning and at times spend a majority of the day at the park for a tournament, but can't make it to a 10:30 a.m. meeting the next day (Sunday) that will only last two hours? We will do everything we can to make sure our kids don't flunk out of school and excel in sports, but not put forth the same effort to make sure our kids don't miss heaven. That will preach!

For those of you who allow your teenager to go to church somewhere else, make sure they are going for the right reasons. As a parent, you should be able to tell if they are spiritually growing and benefiting from it, or if it is just an avenue for them to be away from you and do what they want. As a parent, you have the responsibility of knowing who is ministering to your teenager, the leaders of the particular ministry, their rules and guidelines, and what their beliefs are as a church. It would be foolish not to know these things and allow your children to be exposed to things that you know are not biblical and are filled with compromise. Another consideration is whether your child is going because they are emotionally involved with someone else. If that's the case, they are more than likely not getting anything out of it unless God really gets ahold of them in the mix. This is possible at any given time or place if they themselves allow it. It is best if your child attends the student ministry of your church if one is provided.

## BEING TOO PASSIVE

One of the things that I love about church is that I can look around and know that I am not alone. That encourages me! I know that I am not fighting this battle alone. That I am not walking this out alone. There are other people who have the same struggles that I do and are still there, worshipping the one true God. That pumps me up! Church is designed to help you. It helps you become a better person overall, and even a better parent. Your children need this, your family needs it, and—most importantly—you need it! When the right church is found for your family, get plugged in and become committed to that church. The right church will challenge everyone in your family to be all that they can be for God. It will help shape and mold your family while also telling you the truth. I am tired of hearing about churches that are watering down the gospel and not holding people to a high standard.

Make church a priority in your home, and with God's help and your encouragement your student will grow up and make church a priority in their own personal life and in their own home. Put Him first, and as you model that to others on a daily basis it will be something they would more than likely desire for themselves.

**Modesty for Our Daughters**

This is an area where I really find myself frustrated. If you have a daughter, please read this particular section a couple of times. It bothers me a great deal how so many homes have allowed the world to influence how their young girls dress. I should be able to tell the difference between a young girl who truly loves the Lord and one who lives for this world by the way they dress. They shouldn't look the same. It's hard enough for our teenage guys and even our men to fight the battle of lust outside the church; they shouldn't have to fight it in the church as well. Proverbs 7 sheds some light on the subject of modesty. It is really straightforward and will hit you right between the eyes.

> "I saw among the simple, I noticed among the young men, a youth who had no sense. He was going down

## PARENT'S INITIATIVE

the street near her corner, walking along in the direction of her house at twilight, as the day was fading, as the dark of night set in. Then out came a woman to meet him, dressed like a prostitute and with crafty intent" (Proverbs 7:7–10 NIV).

This woman was dressed like a prostitute. It was what she was wearing that defined what she was looking for. It expressed her purpose for being out there in the middle of the night. It expressed what she desired and spoke of her motives. She was basically telling the whole world that she was available and for sale. She was an object.

We can clearly see the intent of this woman. We know what she has in mind. Yet we do not seem to get the message on this subject clearly today. Nothing has changed here! Today, too many women and young girls don't consider the message they are sending through the way they dress. As long as they feel good about and look good in what they are wearing, it doesn't matter how revealing or short their choices are. Very little thought is put into what others may think or how others may struggle because of these choices. In fact, these ideas are often disregarded in the name of freedom of expression, as if we did not affect each other. We all know this is not the case. Much of the clothes designed today are fashioned to look sexy and revealing. The agenda behind this industry is not a Christian one. Instead, its focus is to sell women as though they were things and not people.

I am sure that most parents don't want to send their daughters out the door to sell their bodies or look like prostitutes, but that's what's happening all over this world. It doesn't help that many female celebrities don't respect themselves and dress inappropriately. Our girls are constantly hearing about how this famous person is so pretty and desired; she is deemed to be beautiful, a worthy object. This message resounds in our culture. The result is that many of our young women think this is the goal. They want to be spoken of in the

## BEING TOO PASSIVE

same light. They want to be viewed with the same approval. They do not see the evil behind all this—for them or others.

We need to take a stand as parents. We should not allow our daughters to dress in a way that sends the wrong message. We are to set the standard and not allow the world to dictate it for us. We can't allow the judgment of others to define us or determine how we allow our daughters to dress.

My pastor says that it's often the parents who buy the clothes for their daughters. Parents complain about how their daughters dress, but they are the ones supporting these choices. Some parents give their girls money and tell them to buy what they want—a foolish practice in so many ways. There is, then, no accountability in what they purchase.

They'd rather not hear their daughters complain, so they compromise. Not only are they compromising, but they are also giving the world an open invitation to come after their daughters. They are saying their girls are available. There are even those who want their daughters to "fit in" or be "popular." Is that really the message you want to send? Are you willing to forsake the reputation of your daughter so she can be "cool" and "accepted"? Do you really want other guys to look at your daughter as if she were an object instead of a real person?

As a father of a young daughter, I am praying that the Lord comes back before she becomes a teenager. If He decides to wait, then so be it. I know this much: Every day my daughter walks out that door, she will be dressed modestly. If what she is wearing isn't acceptable, she is going to change. I don't expect to have problems here because I will be buying her clothes. Some fathers take their daughters shopping and have them model the clothes that they want to purchase. They began doing this with their daughters at a very young age and it just stuck. During this time the fathers tell their daughters whether something is acceptable or not. They are not being controlling. They are protecting, teaching, and preparing their daughters for life.

## PARENT'S INITIATIVE

This also builds relationship through spending time with one another. It shows the importance of setting a standard and not setting the daughter (or others) up for failure. It's so important to communicate why we need standards. Not only is it about pleasing the Lord in our choices, it's also about living wisely in our culture, not sending the wrong message, and protecting the minds of others.

Why would anyone who says they love the Lord willingly set other men up for failure and not care about it? We are to be there for one another and not cause each other to stumble. Some think that shouldn't be an issue for any Christian man; I wish that were the case. Many parents have become passive in this area. They need to wake up and make some changes.

God forbid that anything happens to our daughters, but we set them up for failure if we do not teach and prepare them. In not doing this, we have helped send the wrong message to others who have no clue. Don't send your daughters out that door with the wrong message that they are "available." I am not a fashion expert by any means, but I know our younger and older ladies can dress in a manner that honors the Lord and still allows them to be the beautiful person God created them to be.

### To Be Continued

Dressing properly affects boys as well as girls in the day of skinny jeans and no shirts, and there are other areas that will be covered later that fall under this category. I encourage you to be more aware of additional areas that I may not address. Pray that God will make you more watchful and that He will help you do what is necessary to take action. You are the parent. Don't be part of the problem in enabling your children to miss the mark in being who God has called them to be.

Take the initiative as you see things. Change will not come overnight; it's a process, and the process is never easy. However, you will see change—little by little—in the midst of the process. Stay focused on those small changes, as they will grow and grow. Let them encourage you. Don't give up, and let's work together.

# BEING TOO PASSIVE

## Application Questions for Chapter 6

1. Do you feel that you have a good balance overall when it comes to parenting? If not, what could you do better?
2. In what ways are you passive personally? Do you think this affects you as a parent too? Is this something you really need to change? What further action steps need to be taken?
3. Are you passive when it comes to church? Are you the one who is always coming up with the excuses as to why you need not attend or get involved?
4. Are you passive when it comes to the way you dress? Are you passive in how you may allow your daughter to dress?
5. ACTION STEP: Get out a piece of paper and take a long look at yourself. Are you a passive parent? How? Make a list of the ways you are currently doing this as a parent.

# Chapter 7: Being Too Aggressive

"Fathers, do not aggravate your children, or they will become discouraged" (Colossians 3:21).

When I speak to students, I like to break words down. I want them to fully understand what each word means because they usually have a basic understanding of that word but may never really have taken the time to really get a grasp of it. Doing this can put emphasis on it and even possibly bring new meaning to it. It helps make me look a little smarter too.

Being aggressive means to show too much aggression. I know that doesn't explain much, so let's look at the word *aggression*. Aggression is a strong action taken with the intention to dominate or master. It can be destructive, cause injury, or be hostile, and it is often caused by frustration. That description should cause some kind of inner discomfort. The intention to dominate is not a Christlike approach.

Look at it this way: There are parents out there who have this approach (and mindset) toward their kids. They want to dominate their lives in every way possible. In many ways, they try to live their own lives through their children because of their missed opportunities or past mistakes.

There are a lot of cases in which people have dominating relationships over other people. When freedom is finally found from these types of relationships, these individuals don't know what to do with themselves

## PARENT'S INITIATIVE

because they are so used to being treated as slaves. They don't know how to think for themselves and make decisions.

We are talking about extremes here. Think about it this way, and I am sure you can relate to these points better. Most parents don't want to think that they are parenting badly, yet you have those parents who are just too passive to the point that they are fixing to lose control if they haven't yet already. Then you have these other parents who are so extremely aggressive in the way they parent that once their kids leave the house, all hell breaks loose.

Because their parents were so aggressive, those kids are going to go crazy when they experience an ounce of freedom. I like to call those types of parents "helicopter parents." You may have heard that term before.

These helicopter parents tend to hover around their kids all the time. They are with them constantly. They don't allow them room to breathe or even room to make any mistakes. They are doing everything they can to protect them and try to spend every waking moment with them. Some even try to live their lives through their kids.

Some kids who are raised like this make really stupid decisions once they leave their homes because they were given no freedom at all. Constantly followed by their parents and mastered by them in every way, these kids never learned how to choose for themselves.

Parents need to find a balance. This type of parent needs to allow their sons and daughters to learn some things the hard way. Yes, we need to protect them as much as we can; but we also need to allow them to face difficulty, face some consequences, solve their own problems, and prepare them to face this world.

Too much aggression toward your kids can lead them towards rebellion. There are some parents who are so overbearing that their children become angry. These kids reach a breaking point.

I know a student like this. These parents were taken for the ride of their lives in a short period of time, and my heart truly went out to them. But in some ways, I found myself not sympathetic. Their child

## BEING TOO AGGRESSIVE

had no life and no freedom whatsoever. The parents had obsessively controlled and dominated them. It was not a surprise that things blew up as they did.

Freedom and trust should be earned and can easily be lost when hurtful actions are taken. There should be consequences for certain actions, but there must also be room for grace and forgiveness. This student, in many ways, resented his parents and went off the deep end for a long period of time.

This style of aggressive parenting reminds me of oppression. That is a very strong way to put it, because no parent wants to think that they have reached that point. To be oppressive is to use unjust and cruel control to make someone else do as you wish. Oppression brings a feeling of being weighed down in the mind and even the body.

Looking at it in that light, it makes a lot of sense. When a parent is overly aggressive they can become oppressive toward their own children, and over time the child loses respect for them because even though the child is being taught good ideas, it is being done in an unjust or cruel manner. The parents' high expectations and cruel use of authority oppress the child. The parents' goals are unrealistic and begin to weigh the child down, hurting them mentally. The children basically live in fear and may end up doing something they will live to regret.

King Solomon in Ecclesiastes shared a lot of wisdom when it came to life's problems. This particular book in the Bible may seem depressing at times, but it gives a lot of insight and reflection on many subjects we struggle with today. Ultimately, the last chapter is the one we should focus on; it deals with oppression and how difficult it can be for someone that is oppressed.

> "Again, I observed all the oppression that takes place under the sun. I saw the tears of the oppressed, with no one to comfort them. The oppressors have great power, and their victims are helpless" (Ecclesiastes 4:1).

# PARENT'S INITIATIVE

My parents were in no way oppressive to me or my sister. They were aggressive at times when it came to disciplining us, but not very often. I cannot imagine how difficult it is for the children or teenagers who have to deal with this type of parenting. They may feel like they have nowhere to turn. They have no one to comfort them. Their parents obviously have authority over them, but they are helpless because they are more of a victim than a child.

To be overly aggressive about things can easily lead to oppression and cause a wedge between you and your children and, at times, even your spouse. It can even cause damage that will take a lot of time to heal. I find myself at times thinking that I may need to relax on some things, whether it's due to the reaction I get from my kids when I discipline them or my wife giving me "the look" after I discipline our kids. I don't want my kids to resent me or be afraid of me. I want to make sure that I have a valid reason for the way I do things and that it is not because of my own insecurities or frustrations. I always want my children to understand why I do as I do and not keep them guessing.

If you are an aggressive parent, you probably know it by now. You may need to take some time for serious personal reflection. Try talking to others close to you. Pray and read your Bible, asking for forgiveness. We have a responsibility to raise our kids and exercise the authority God has given us, but we are not to abuse it. To be oppressive does not reflect the character of Jesus, and we are supposed to be a reflection of Him in all we do. It is not easy, but it's something that we should be striving for. With His help we can make the changes that are necessary.

## Fighting Battles for Your Kids

We are living in a time when parents are constantly fighting battles for their children. In the past, parents allowed their kids to fight a lot of their own battles and were very selective about when to step in. Those battles were the ones that shaped their children's character and prepared them for the future. Today, parents are calling schools to argue with teachers about the way subjects are being taught or because their child is

# BEING TOO AGGRESSIVE

failing, especially when their child is not doing what they are supposed to be doing.

Today, parents argue with coaches because their child is not getting any playing time when their student is not a good player at that sport in the first place. Parents are calling colleges to argue with professors because their young adult is failing that class. These are all examples of being too aggressive and not allowing your child to grow. These kids are not learning how to deal with the difficulties they will face in the future. These parents are trying to be in control as much as they can. This will not bear good fruit.

## A Biblical Example of Aggression

The story of Joash in 2 Chronicles 22:11–24:27 gives us an example of what happens when parents make all the decisions for their children and do not teach them skills for wise decision-making when they come of age. Joash was given great advice, but he never grew up. This young ruler became so dependent on what he was told that his effectiveness hinged on the advice he received from his advisers.

His story is one that isn't easy to accept. When he was just one year old, his grandmother cleaned house and decided to kill his family for power. Luckily, he got away and was rescued by his uncle and aunt. His uncle was a priest, a fact that allowed them to hide him for six years in the temple. When the opportune time came, Joash was crowned king. As Joash was a young king, his uncle made all the decisions (which was probably wise); yet his uncle wasn't going to live forever because he was well advanced in age.

When it came to Joash running the kingdom on his own, he didn't know what to do other than listen to his advisers; and his advisers didn't have the best advice because they were evil. They did not have a relationship with God as his uncle had. The advice that he received led to the death of his uncle's son and his army's defeat in battle. In the end, he was assassinated by his own officials.

# PARENT'S INITIATIVE

Because of the aggression of his uncle, Joash never learned the importance of depending on God for himself. His uncle was a priest of God, but he did not do a good job of instilling some important values and principles in the young boy. Joash only knew how to follow his uncle; his knowledge of God was only secondhand. He did not establish a strong relationship with God himself that would protect him from bad advice.

## A Firsthand Example of Aggression

Here are a couple of examples that I have seen firsthand of both extremes. I know of two young men who are in their mid to late twenties and are still living at home. In both settings, you have a set of parents that are either too passive or too aggressive in raising their children.

One of them made a serious mistake and is not able to drive because of it. This young man has a college degree and seems to have enough sense to be living on his own. He had his own business once and was beginning to see some success. He has a great heart and is trying his best to walk out his relationship with God, but his parents always get in the way of his growth. I received an e-mail from his mother defending him following a situation involving him and another individual in our church.

He is in his late twenties, and his mom is still fighting some of his battles. His parents have always felt sorry for him because he has gone through so much because of the decisions he has made. They are trying their best to help him out, but all they are doing is enabling him more each day. They allowed too much, and he has really never been on his own except for when he was off to college. After he received his degree, he went back to his safe haven, his home. I hate to say it, but he may never be on his own and learn to truly function without someone helping him.

The other young man is in his midtwenties. You can look at him and know that there is something wrong. Even so, I have been around him for several years and can see that he could function on his own and has more sense than most give him credit for.

## BEING TOO AGGRESSIVE

Our church has embraced him, and we have done more to build his character than a lot of other people in his life. Other churches have asked him not to come back because of his shortcomings. He has a short temper and problems getting along with others.

I have had several run-ins with his mom because he would run to her every time he had a problem with the way we attempted to keep him accountable. He would either do or say something that needed to be addressed, and when we addressed it he did not like it. We have asked him to take a break from ministries in our church, but we never told him he couldn't come back to church.

Over the years, I have seen him mature a lot. We strived to find a balance with him, and we are very consistent. It would be safe to say that we have been more consistent with him than anyone else has. His temper has gotten the best of him at times, but over time it has gotten better. He's also getting along better with others. He still has his moments, but they have become less frequent.

One of his main problems is his mother. She has always felt sorry for him. His father died while he was young, and he really didn't have a father figure in his life. He never fought his own battles because his mom always fought them for him. He has a problem with responsibility because his mom has always done things for him and hasn't taken the time to teach him.

She is now trying to implement some things in his life and having a huge problem with it. She was a "helicopter parent," and now she can't get rid of him. I have talked to her several times as she cried on the phone; over and over again I have given her the best advice I could, but she still feels sorry for him and enables him. She gives him money repeatedly and really hasn't taught him how to budget the money he makes from working. He has been known to have several jobs and lose them because of his temper.

We are currently doing our best to help him. Several men in our church have taken it upon themselves to teach him. We don't lecture him, because he is an adult and we treat him that way. We are consistent with him and we don't easily give in to him and his tactics. Let's just say that over the years, he has learned how to work the system. He has grown and continues to do so. We have found a balance and we have kept at it. When we need to be stern, we are; when we need to offer grace, we do. Because we haven't given up on him, it has helped him even more to mature.

My son just recently got in trouble at school. Of course, he has a different interpretation of it. He said it wasn't his fault and the teacher really did not give him a chance to explain. I could have let it slide and reasoned with him. He provided a good case. Then I thought about it and realized that would have been too passive. The fact remains that he got in trouble. He received some discipline and instruction.

His current teacher is not one to just discipline kids or not show mercy because she is having a bad day. I am sure she allows things to slide here and there and takes mental notes throughout the day. She is not too aggressive, either, because I have seen her in action on a field trip. She is the real deal and a great teacher. She has found a balance and is consistent. She does run a tight ship in her classroom, but she is one of the best in her school.

It's sad to know that there are parents who find themselves taking their aggression out on their kids because of their own circumstances and pasts. If I were a teacher, it would be hard for me to find a balance. Just imagine what most teachers have to deal with and how their style clashes with the way parents do their own thing.

Parents come in all sorts of shapes and sizes, and they are all shaped by their experience: a bad day at work, a rotten mood, being too tired, or even just having a bad past—those experiences affect them. Their past may have been full of verbal, physical, or even sexual abuse. A bad upbringing can cause parents to act aggressively, but that is not fair to the child. If you feel that is the case for you, you should seek some counseling and, most importantly, pray about it. Ask God to heal you and help you to forgive. Forgetting what has been done can be very hard, but forgiving what has been done and said to you can be accomplished and is the key to freedom and a better life. I know firsthand how hard

## BEING TOO AGGRESSIVE

it is to forget the past, but forgiving has been a lot easier. We all will have our moments as parents and we will make mistakes. We must use diligence to not take out our personal aggression out on our own kids. Ephesians 4:31 says that we should get rid of all bitterness, rage, anger, harsh words, and slander, as well as all types of evil behavior.

In the midst of being too aggressive, you can often find bitterness because of the past. Rage, anger, and harsh words can be the result of oppression experienced as a child. Maybe it wasn't as extreme as oppression, but there was a lot of aggression in your home while you were growing up. We need to deal with it and get rid of it so that it will not affect our own kids. Ephesians 4:32 says that we should be kind to each other, tenderhearted, forgiving one another, just as God through Christ has forgiven us. That's how we can take care of it.

Parenting may become easier if the authority that has been extended to us is not abused or dispensed in an unfair manner. It will become even easier if we address past issues that linger deep in our minds and hearts. As the past is addressed and dealt with, we will be given the ability to forgive, and be kind and tenderhearted not only to those in our homes over which we have authority, but to everyone we come in contact with.

In no way am I saying that discipline should not be given, but a balance has to be found between being too passive and being too aggressive. Finding a balance is one of the hardest things to do. As a parent, I constantly strive for a balance in raising my kids. I can be too passive and lead my kids on a path that is going to lead them in the wrong direction. I can be too aggressive, so that when they get a taste of freedom it will leave them unprepared to face the real world.

It all comes down to being aware, not being foolish, and not turning a blind eye to things that need to be addressed. To offer grace when needed and discipline when needed is vital. To not be closed-minded and act like we know what we are doing when confronted by others that are trying to help makes sense, especially when it comes from those that you have seen live out their relationship with God, those who have already paid their dues by raising a great strong family—those who are good parents.

## PARENT'S INITIATIVE

Find a balance and don't be too passive or too aggressive. I will touch on how we can be too aggressive in disciplining our children in a later chapter. With God's help, countless prayers, listening to the advice of others, and offering grace when needed and discipline when needed, we will find that balance.

### Application Questions for Chapter 7

1. Are you too aggressive as a parent? If so, how?
2. If you are too aggressive, do you think that has possibly affected your child in being rebellious? What could you do to improve?
3. Would you be categorized as a helicopter parent? If so, in what ways? How can you avoid that from now on?
4. Do you fight your kids' battles? If so, in what ways? How can you work on letting go of this habit?
5. ACTION STEP: If you answered yes to question number 1, do something to change this pattern. Pray about it, and then call your pastor or a close friend and ask for help. Allow God to minister to your heart about this. It will change your life.

## Chapter 8: Relationships

> "Always be humble and gentle. Be patient with each other, making allowance for each other's faults because of your love. Make every effort to keep yourselves united in the Spirit, binding yourselves together with peace" (Ephesians 4:2–3).

My wife was hosting an event for the girls in our student ministry along with some of our adult leaders. It was a "Girls Night In," and they just hung out, ate junk food, played games, and did pedicures. They really had a great time hanging out and building relationships. My wife just happened to be giving a pedicure to one of the girls and just talking about things in general. Out of nowhere, this girl made a comment that broke my wife's heart. She said she had never had a pedicure. She had begged her mom to take her, and she would not. She mentioned how her mother was willing to spend money on herself but not on her and went on to say that her mom really never spent time with her at all. Now I know students have a tendency to exaggerate, but this girl said this with such sincerity that my wife had a hard time not believing her.

It would seem that this young girl genuinely wanted a relationship with her mom. She was yearning to do those things that moms and daughters typically do. And this girl is not the only one. She is one of many young girls all over the world who need attention from their parents. Many of the students I know wish they had a better relationship with their parents. Kids desire and need that.

# PARENT'S INITIATIVE

We were created for companionship. Growing up and feeling alone has to be one of the hardest things for anyone. Especially for a young teenager who doesn't know who they are yet! They will cling to anyone who shows them any type of affection. If they don't have a strong relationship with their parents, they will find an outlet somewhere else and allow those relationships to mold them. That is exactly what is happening in the lives of many teenagers today. If they are not getting love at home, they will find it somewhere else. If they don't feel like they have a place in their own home, they will find another home. I have seen this firsthand time and time again.

There are key relationships in every home, and I would like to think that there is a priority list that everyone should follow. You may want to follow this and make it your priority list too. This is how I go about my relationships.

## Relationship #1: God

> "Jesus replied, '"You must love the Lord your God with all your heart, all your soul, and all your mind." This is the first and greatest commandment'" (Matthew 22:37–38).

This is the number one relationship in my home and in my family. When my relationship with Jesus is strong, other relationships in my life are strong too. When my relationship with Him is suffering, other relationships in my life will suffer as well. I have noticed that as I have drawn closer to Him, it has made me a better person, husband, father, family member, friend, and minister. My relationship with Him is always evolving; it is a process, a process that will never end. I will never be perfect, but I am striving toward that every day.

Every parent needs to make their relationship with God number one. That needs to be vocalized and shown by example. Children need to see their parents spending time in prayer; they need to see them worshipping; and they need to see their parents have their priorities in order.

# RELATIONSHIPS

As they see your example, they will understand that following God is not about being perfect. It's about striving to grow closer to Him each day, to show love, grace, mercy, compassion, forgiveness, and more of His attributes to others. Your kids will be drawn to that. If you are not truly close to Jesus, you will not able to show them those things. If you are simply religious and live hypocritically, your kids will see that instead. As a result, they will not be drawn to you or God because of that hypocrisy. We can never fool our own children. They are constantly around us, watching our every move. We should be above reproach and do our best to set a godly example for them because we love them so much.

The end goal for all parents is to be able to say what Paul said with complete confidence: "Follow my example as I follow the example of Christ" (1 Corinthians 11:1 NIV).

I read a book in which the author explained how his research had found the dynamic of how our relationship with God sets the example for our kids. They will live their lives according to the way we lived our lives before their eyes. Through his research he came across an article that basically said that we can thank our parents for all of our problems. This article went on to explain how our own parents contributed about twenty-three thousand chromosomes to us. A lot of what we inherit is easy to recognize because we look like our parents in different ways. Yet that's not all that we picked up from them! Most people end up worshipping whatever god their parents worshipped.

Psychologists would call this the "law of exposure." This law basically states that our lives are determined by our thoughts, and our thoughts are determined by what we are exposed to. Ultimately our minds absorb and reflect what we experience the most. It shouldn't surprise us that we have a tendency to worship the gods of our fathers and mothers.

For example, if it's more important for a father to be successful in his career, and his life revolves around that, that's what his kids will be exposed to and they will see that he is willing to sacrifice his days off and even family vacations because he is so focused on his career. He works

## PARENT'S INITIATIVE

endless hours and is always "stuck" in the office. Either his kids will resent it, or they'll want the same thing and neglect their families in the same manner one day. They will also see what "god" their father truly serves. He is serving the "god" of success and is willing to do whatever it takes to get it. Instead of finding their identity or worth in God, they will try to find it the way their father did for all those years. They will seek success first before God Himself and be willing to sacrifice their family along the way as well. Just like their father did.

Then there is the mom who is more concerned about keeping up with everyone around her. She is very focused on how things look and wants everything to seem perfect, when it's far from it. Everything has its place and serves its purpose in her home. A lot of time and money is spent trying to keep up with the Joneses. Huge amounts of money are budgeted for clothes, upgrades on the house, the "right" car, and so on. Her identity is not found in God but in her acceptance by those around her and how they perceive her family. To keep that just right, she expends her energy to make the "perfect" family in the eyes of others.

So it boils down to this. What we worship, idolize, or make a priority in our homes will more than likely be the same for our kids. There are many other examples, but it's vital that you take a few moments to reflect on this. The path that we choose for our homes will probably be chosen by our kids when they have a home and family of their own.

Our children are looking to us for their identity in God. What we put on a pedestal, they will too. Most students' passion for God often matches that of their parents. There are those students who are more passionate for the things of God, unlike their parents, but that is not the norm.

Parents usually set the "spiritual temperature" in their homes. That means that we have a huge responsibility in our choices and in what we model to our children. If we want them to be hungry for the things of God, we must make sure that we exhibit a deep hunger for the things of God too. My personal goal as a parent is to do everything I can to make sure that my children have access to God and are being raised in a home that has a great example of how to walk out a sincere relationship with

# RELATIONSHIPS

God. I want to be able to stand before God and know I did my best to represent Him in my home.

## Relationship #2: Your Spouse

> "Husbands, love your wives, just as Christ loved the church and gave himself up for her to make her holy, cleansing her by the washing with water through the word, and to present her to himself as a radiant church, without stain or wrinkle or any other blemish, but holy and blameless. In this same way, husbands ought to love their wives as their own bodies. He who loves his wife loves himself. After all, no one ever hated their own body, but they feed and care for their body, just as Christ does the church—for we are members of his body" (Ephesians 5:25–30 NIV).

This is the second relationship that we must build up on a daily basis. If you are not currently married, please continue to read because there is value in this. Kids need to see a strong and healthy relationship between their parents. If you are not married or are recently divorced, there still needs to be a strong relationship between father and mother if it's possible. This relationship is so out in the open; they see it all the time, and it helps mold them. They will handle their own relationships in their lives in the same way this one is handled. This is especially true of when they get to the place where they are ready to look for that person they are going to spend the rest of their life with.

I see students being disrespectful to their parents all the time; and these parents wonder why they are being treated so. Then I see how the parents treat one another, and I find my answer. Don't you think that if kids see their parents disrespecting one another that they will think it is okay for them as well? If Mom can talk to Dad like that, why can't I? If Dad treats Mom like that, why can't I? This will happen in the home and outside the home. Eventually, they will treat their spouses, or even the opposite sex in general, in like manner.

## PARENT'S INITIATIVE

I am not perfect by any means, and my marriage will show that. You may know me personally and remember an instance where I fell short in this area. I try my best to be respectful to my wife, especially when I am in front of my kids. I try my best to love my wife and show her affection in front of my kids. I don't allow my son to speak to my wife in a disrespectful way, and I always have her back. If your kids have any sense of disunity, they will use it to their advantage. If you are not intentional about being united as parents, your kids will quickly learn how to divide you to try to get what they want!

Kids know how to work the system. They know when there is disunity. They know when there is a problem. A mother recently made a comment in front of another lady in our church that made it very obvious why she was having problems in her home. As this mother was speaking to the other lady, her daughter walked up. The mother stopped to look at what her daughter was wearing. She did not get upset about it, but told her daughter to make sure she did not wear that around her father because she knew he did not want her to dress that way. That statement completely undermined her husband and taught her daughter that it was okay to go against her father's wishes and disrespect his authority. Not only will she do this to her dad, but to her future husband as well. She is teaching her child to hide things and undermine one of the authority figures God placed in her life.

On another occasion, we were hosting an event at our house one night and I overheard a conversation that two girls were having. They were talking about the outfit one of the girls had worn that morning at church. One said there was no way that she would have worn that because it was inappropriate and too short. The other girl said that she did not care if it was inappropriate; she liked the way she looked in it. She said her mom did not want her to wear it, but her dad said it was okay to wear for church. That is just another example of a child who knows how to work the system.

It is so important that our children see a strong and healthy relationship between their parents. Not a perfect one, but a strong and healthy one. It should be a relationship that is united in serving Jesus

# RELATIONSHIPS

and honors and respects one another. This requires that we put God first in our own personal lives and then in our marriages.

## Your Marriage Changes Your Kids

Sociological and biological studies have a few things to say about how a marriage affects a child's development. 1) As an infant, the lack of development of children's attention abilities, impulse control, motor skills, and high-level thinking has been traced back to stress experienced in an instable home. 2) As a student, kids from a stable home are statistically more likely to stay in school, have fewer behavioral issues, and finish higher education. 3) Emotionally, kids with married parents are less vulnerable to emotional illness, depression, and suicide.

There is an author who is a molecular biologist and devoted to family development. He mentioned how he always has parents coming up to him and asking him for the key to being better parents. He always answers their question by saying that the most important thing parents can do for their kids is go home and love their spouse.

## Relationship #3: Kids

A parent's relationship with their children comes third. If you are married, this doesn't come second or even first. Some parents regard their children as priority one. That is not good because God should be first. I love my kids a lot, but they don't come before God or my wife. My wife understands that God is first, she is second, my kids are third, and everyone/everything else follows . This order actually brings success to them all.

The best way to get to know someone is by spending time with them and investing effort in that relationship. My relationship with God has become stronger based on the time that I have spent with Him. It's the same with our kids. If we want to get to know our children, we must spend time with them. Do some of the things they enjoy, and then have them spend time with you doing the things you enjoy.

# PARENT'S INITIATIVE

We have a missionary friend who went to watch a dance recital with his daughter one day and the next day went shooting guns. That's a pretty cool trade-off. Quality time together will be something your kids will never forget and will build lasting memories.

My father and I really didn't spend a lot of quality time together, but I will never forget the time when he took me fishing. I was probably around ten years old, and I really had a blast with him. We did take family vacations and watched wrestling and movies together quite a bit. Yet, I remember more than anything that one time when it was just me and him under that bridge and we fished for hours.

I did not like baiting the hook and he did it for me every time. He would drop his pole and bait mine. I got snagged on the rocks a couple of times and he didn't get frustrated about freeing my hook. The weather was awesome! It was a perfect day for fishing. The only thing he was a little upset about was that I caught more fish than he did. He still denies it to this day. That day I felt close to my dad; and to this day, I remember that day like it was yesterday.

Your kids long for those moments. They should not be rare occasions; they should happen on a regular basis. I am trying to work on this with my son and daughter by taking advantage of the opportunities I am given, even creating them and being intentional in those moments. I don't just want one moment; I want many moments etched in their memories.

If I don't have this time with them, someone else will come along and take it instead. There will come a time when it will be too late; and if I have not done this, I will regret not investing that time and building those relationships. Invest time with your kids and do what you can to build a relationship with them. Don't let your job, daily stress, tiredness, or even selfishness get in the way of spending time with your family.

## Your Children Don't Need another Friend; They Need a Parent

Many parents today are more concerned with being a friend to their child than with being a parent. I often see and hear of parents who have abdicated parenting for being a friend instead. A friend is someone

# RELATIONSHIPS

attached to another by affection or esteem. A parent is a person who raises and cares for another. They are different relationships.

Most people only have a couple of true friends. You know: someone you can really trust. You know they will always be honest with you, even when it hurts. Usually some kind of conflict has taken place during this friendship and it has just solidified the relationship even more. You probably have other friends in which the relationship is not that solid too. Most of us have more of these relationships than we do the other. These "friends" will not be honest with you and will do or say anything to make sure that things are always "cool"; they are surface relationships. Conflict are avoided at all times, and compromise is always present.

Many parents have this kind of less-confrontational relationship with their kids. They allow their kids to get away with just about anything because they want to win their affection or esteem. They want to be accepted and don't want any kind of conflict. In their eyes, it's just easier that way. You will hardly ever hear the word "no" come out of their mouths.

They will even go so far as to attempt to be like their kids and not the adult they are called to be. They will dress like them, talk like them, hang out with them, watch what they watch, and listen to what they listen to, and so on—but they will not protect them and challenge them to be the individuals God has called them to be. They have no real standards set and do not share a strong commitment to Jesus Christ either. These types of parents will "like" their statuses on social media when they shouldn't and brag about taking a survey there that says they are a "cool" parent.

This is not what it means to be a parent. A parent has the responsibility to bring up and care for their child. Real parents say "no" when necessary. Real parents protect their children from the potential harm around them and do not set them up for failure. Christian parents are called to raise their kids with morals and standards so that they will not end up like the "world." When a parent decides to be a friend, they will have a great struggle when it comes time to discipline their children. Parents are called to set the standard in their homes, not allow their kids to set it.

## PARENT'S INITIATIVE

They are called to raise their kids and not let their kids raise themselves or allow the world to raise them.

When I was a student pastor, I wanted to be the pastor that I would want my own kids to be under. I want their pastor to be "real" with them and hold them to a high standard, keep them accountable, and teach them the important principles found in the Word of God. I don't necessarily want them to be "entertained," but I do want them to be challenged. I obviously want them to enjoy church, but I also want them to have the opportunity to truly experience the power and presence of God. I don't want them to have just another adult "friend."

I try to look at our students as my own kids. It may not have always been popular, but I know that there will come a day when former students will come to my wife and me and thank us. There are a lot of ministries that are going about it the wrong way, and they will have to answer for it. In the same way, many parents will have to answer for their decisions one day as well, if they haven't already.

Once I got a text message from a parent who was having a lot of trouble with their student at home. It did not surprise me to get this text because I had seen what they were letting this kid get away with. They gave him just about anything and let him do what he wanted. He was disrespectful to his mom and dad. My wife has seen him at random places that he really should not have been by himself. His parents just dropped him off at these locations on school nights and gave him a lot of money to blow on candy and drinks or whatever else he could get his hands on. He was not even out of junior high yet and already had way too much freedom. His mother was really disappointed in him. He had been very disrespectful toward her, and she had had enough.

It was kind of crazy how everything unfolded as we texted back and forth. She was practically answering herself in the same manner I was going to answer her. It made it a lot easier on me because I was determined to be blunt with her. It finally hit her, and she realized what she was doing. She realized that she was more of a friend then a parent. She realized that all this time she had felt sorry for him because of a family illness. She had allowed him to get away with anything or do

# RELATIONSHIPS

anything he wanted as a result. She also saw that she had allowed other things to take priority in their lives and put God and church on the back burner. She went on to thank me, and I really don't know what for. I was thankful that God had shown her that she was more of a friend than a parent.

## A Dad and His Daughter

These relationships are important, and it's up to us to work on them. God has more than likely already been dealing with you in some relational areas.

Every relationship dynamic is important and matters. A relationship between mother and son is important, just as it is between mother and daughter and father and son. I briefly want to hit on another relationship that is also very important; I will discuss it again later too. A daughter needs to know that she is are loved by her father. A best-selling author said that fathers bring something different to the table that many mothers cannot. The biggest mistake dads make is in not understanding their significance.

In many ways fathers help their daughters with self-confidence, body image, education, career, and romantic relationships. All these areas are key areas in raising a daughter to become the woman God has called her to be. Daughters need their dad's affection and attention. If she does not get that affection from her dad, she will attempt to get it from another male. Trust me: most girls will have no problem finding a male who is more than willing to give her the attention and affection she is longing for.

If a father is not present in your daughter's life, do what you can to have a "father figure" in her life, someone who is trustworthy and truly loves the Lord. I have personally seen and known many girls who were looking for love in the worst ways, and most of the time I could see why. Their own fathers were either absent from their lives or not giving their daughters the love and the attention they needed. Fathers need to man up and be the fathers God has called them to be.

# PARENT'S INITIATIVE

## A Moment I Will Never Forget

I am not a super-emotional person, but I do believe God is working on me in that department. I noticed it the day I took my son to the movies. During the previews, I noticed this guy was standing and eating what seemed to be nachos and cheese. He was also interacting with two other people who were sitting there. It was dark and hard to see what was going on. This guy was doing this all the way through the previews. I finally saw what he was doing: he was actually feeding these individuals the nachos and cheese. Then the brightness from the screen hit just right, and I realized that the individuals he was feeding were quadriplegics.

I am not sure if they were his kids or if he was working as a caregiver. He clearly enjoyed what he was doing and was spending time with them. Let's just say that they were his kids. Think about how the rest of his life would be spent caring for these individuals. Think about the time that is going to be spent. How grateful will these individuals be to this guy who was standing there feeding them nachos and cheese? How grateful are they that this man is there with them to give them a drink of their soda? I am sure this man enjoyed the movie as well, but he was also there to serve these individuals who were going to spend the rest of their lives in wheelchairs. It was a living picture of love and truly caring for someone. That is relationship. It really broke my heart to see this and almost brought me to tears.

Relationships are vital in our everyday lives. We all long for some kind of relationship, and at times we will do whatever we can to get it. I want to encourage you to work on every relationship in your life. Don't let other things take priority. Work on these every day and don't give up. People will go to great lengths to get what they want and may even compromise to get it. We were created to be in relationship; and if those closest to you are not getting it from you, they may try to fill that void through other relationships. If their priorities are not right, then they will go find that relationship they long for in someone or something else.

Spending time with your family is not time wasted; spending time with your family is an investment. At times, we can look at spending

## RELATIONSHIPS

time with our families as a chore and not as an opportunity to make a difference and really create some moments. It's the small things we do with our families that they will remember more than anything else.

### Application Questions for Chapter 8

1. Make an honest assessment: What are the priority of relationships in your home? Would your spouse and children agree with your list?
2. If you are divorced, do you honor and respect your ex-spouse at all times? Have you been guilty of throwing them under the bus in front of your kids or others in the past?
3. How are you intentionally investing in your relationships? With God? Your spouse? Your children? Could you improve in any of these relationships? How?
4. How can you work on being united in parenting?
5. Fathers, are you being intentional with your daughter? If not, what can you do better? Would you be willing to ask someone to keep you accountable in this area?
6. ACTION STEP: Ask your spouse if they can honestly say that you respect and honor them at all times. If not, what could you do better?

# Chapter 9: Entertainment

"I will lead a life of integrity in my own home.
I will refuse to look at anything vile and vulgar"
(Psalm 102:2–3).

This is an area in which many Christians, parents, and homes have become too relaxed. For the longest time I was one of those individuals who watched and listened to just about anything. I did not really think twice about it. Growing up, we watched movies as a family. It was normal in our home to watch about three movies a week. A lot of them weren't what you would call "family friendly," but one thing my parents did make sure of was that I covered my eyes when a suggestive scene came on. They did not consider language a big deal.

When it came to music, I listened to just about anything I wanted. I remember listening to all sorts of music. The only genre of music I really never got into was country because I found it too depressing at times.

Let's put it this way: There wasn't any accountability. I had a job and bought what I wanted. I could bring anything in the house without any concern. No one was going to ask about what I had. When I was a teenager in the early to late '90s, I noticed a strong cultural shift had begun to take place.

A concern over teaching the importance of setting a standard and even the importance of protecting your home lessened. It was like the older generation was naive to what was going on. We weren't taught how we could easily allow the Enemy access into our homes by the way we entertained ourselves.

## PARENT'S INITIATIVE

While I was a teenager, the Internet was just becoming "the" thing to have in your home. Having it was a big deal, and we were one of the few in our neighborhood who had it. I remember the days of dial-up connections: as you turned on your computer, you heard a dial tone and all these buzzing and ringing sounds just to connect to the Internet. It was a process, and took time, but that wasn't a big deal. We were willing to wait for it. Today it is another story. Everything has to be instant.

I am sure that most parents back then were not aware of what their kids had access to and how easily a child could find themselves looking at something they had no business looking at. Just the misspelling of a word or innocently looking up something could lead them to a website that they weren't intending to see. I was one of those who accidentally accessed porn on the Internet.

I was not taught about how what you allow to come into you was going to come out. I did not know that the way I entertained myself would influence me in many other ways. It influenced the way I thought, talked, acted, how I treated others, and how I went on to treat and look at the opposite sex; it even affected my relationship with Christ. To be honest with you, I really didn't get ahold of this until several years after being married. I hate to admit that, but it's the truth. Over time I did choose more appropriate things to watch, but there was still a lot of compromise.

In the homes of many families, there is a lot of compromise and little accountability. Parents allow their kids to watch and listen to just about anything they like and later wonder why there is so much turmoil in their homes. We fail to see how our choices are connected. We need to connect the dots. I read once (and cannot remember the source) that if our daily routines are feeding our flesh, then we will grow to love those things. If we are feeding our spirit like we should be, then we will be who we are to be. Our homes will be as they ought to be; our relationships will be as they should be; our family will be as it should be; and so on down the line. This is a valid and powerful point. Everyone has an appetite for something, and it is all about how we are feeding it. How, as a parent, are you feeding your home?

# ENTERTAINMENT

> "And now, dear brothers and sisters, one final thing. Fix your thoughts on what is true, and honorable, and right, and pure, and lovely, and admirable. Think about things that are excellent and worthy of praise" (Philippians 4:8).

We must always consider whether what we are taking in honors God or not. This may seem a little extreme, but it is not. Are your choices in life more about you or more about Him? When you are focused on pleasing Him, you are more careful about what influences you in your personal life and in your home. When you are investing in what you want, you will watch, listen, and read whatever you want and not think twice about it, even though it may *damn* God several times or fill you with lustful thoughts.

Many parents wonder why they have the problems they have, and yet they don't take steps to protect their homes. Many individuals wonder why they struggle in certain ways, yet they are not making the necessary sacrifices in those areas to protect themselves. It's all about feeding your appetite. Let's break it down this way.

> "Then I will live among the people of Israel and be their God, and they will know that I am the Lord their God. I am the one who brought them out of the land of Egypt so that I could live among them. I am the Lord their God" (Exodus 29:45–46).

When it comes to your home, can it be said that God lives among you in your home? When it comes to the way you entertain yourself, can it be said that God is among that? Can people who come to your home know that God is welcome there? When people spend time with you, do they know that God is with you because of the music you listen to or what you choose to watch? Those are questions that we should take a few moments and reflect on.

God has blessed me in so many ways. He actually lives with me. I want to honor Him in all I do. I am working on this daily and letting

# PARENT'S INITIATIVE

go of things that will cause God to not want to live with me. He can't reside in an individual or a home that is full of compromise, where He is not welcome.

> "Dear friends, if we deliberately continue sinning after we received knowledge of the truth, there is no longer any sacrifice that will cover these sins" (Hebrews 10:26).

## What's the Big Deal?

I have spent a lot of time around students. They have a way of simply confessing what they do at home. They often find themselves in a group, just talking to friends, and they freely share what they watch on TV, the music they listen to, and so on. In some situations the parents have no clue what their kids are doing to entertain themselves; others are very much aware.

It is every parent's responsibility to do what they can to be in the "know" and aware of what's going on in the entertainment world. If you do not stay current, you will have no idea what you are allowing your kids to bring into your home. That means you are not protecting your home as God has called you to do. Parents have the responsibility of knowing what is entering in their homes. It is your sanctuary.

What I find really difficult to understand is that many times, the worldly music, movies, and books that some of our students had were purchased by their parents. Many of those parents went as far as to watch, listen, and read them along with their kids. These parents are allowing their kids to set the standard for their home and are not using discernment in their choices. Bad seed will bear bad fruit.

Everything that comes into our home influences our kids. I remember having a meeting with a student. He was having some dramatic experiences and claimed to be hearing voices that were telling him to do bad things. He went on to say that he had also seen a physical form from which these voices emanated, and that if he did not do the evil things this entity told him to do, the entity would attempt to hurt him. You

## ENTERTAINMENT

could tell that this experience had traumatized him. I just kept asking questions in the direction of what else he was doing and watching.

He finally told me he had watched a movie that involved paranormal activity with his parents as a family. This movie contained the following: 1) A couple of suggestive sexual scenes in which a couple was filming themselves having sex (with no nudity). 2) Several demonic scenes and people "teasing" these demonic influences. 3) At least sixteen F-words and several other curses. 4) The Lord's name was taken in vain nine times.

> "I will be careful to live a blameless life—when will you come to help me? I will lead a life of integrity in my own home. I will refuse to look at anything vile and vulgar. I hate all who deal crookedly; I will have nothing to do with them. I will reject perverse ideas and stay away from every evil" (Psalm 101:2–4).

Here is something to really think about. Have you ever sat down with your family to watch a movie like this? Is this a movie to watch with your family? This student was probably fourteen at the time, and this movie was rated R. I can guarantee that this movie had a profound influence on his life, and definitely not for the good. In fact, it opened a door into his life and was one of the reasons he was going through this traumatic time. It led him into other things. He also confessed that he had been using a Ouija board.

His mom first approached me with his problems and asked someone on staff to sit down and talk to him about these recent events. She was broken by this and was having a lot of problems with him. She had seen him standing in the yard outside, arguing with someone she could not see. She had even gone as far as to lock herself and her other kids in the bedroom out of fear of what he would do because he was so angry at times. Unfortunately, she and her husband brought some of this on themselves through their choices. It's difficult to say that, but it is true. There is no telling what else they may have watched as a family.

## PARENT'S INITIATIVE

It is a sad fact that families are sitting down and watching garbage together on a regular basis. This applies to all media. Parents allow their kids to watch inappropriate TV programs too. These movies, TV shows, books, and songs promote a lot of ungodly ideas. Ideas have consequences. When we allow them in our homes, we (and our children) are subjected to them. It's a big deal. These influences are powerful and hurting us in ways we don't even realize.

To be influenced is to be under the act or power of something or someone producing an effect without an apparent exertion of force or direct exercise of command. Take a second to read this description of what it is to be influenced again.

This is exactly what is taking place in the lives of many students. They are being influenced so much by this world that they don't even realize it at times. The things they are allowed to partake of are having influence in their lives. They are influencing them in how they think, talk, act, and treat others. The areas in which many parents have the most problems with in their children can be directly traced to what they have allowed in their homes.

Our children's pastor overheard a conversation that one kid was having with another kid. They were talking about an extremely violent movie that also included a lot of sexual situations with nudity. It's definitely not a movie that you should sit and watch with a six-year-old. Yet a father and son sat down and watched it; the young boy was boasting about it. Even though he may have covered his son's eyes during the sexual scenes, or even fast-forwarded through them, sitting there and watching it says you condone and support it. Parents are opening their homes to garbage.

We have a responsibility to guard our homes. We are supposed to check up on things and look into what is being allowed. Parents have a responsibility to protect their kids. I know kids will sneak around and do their thing sometimes, but we need to have an idea of where they are at and who they are with. It's not about giving them space or learning how to make right decisions. Your kids don't fully develop the decision-making part of the brain until they are young adults. They need their

# ENTERTAINMENT

parents to guide them, help them to make the right choices, and keep them accountable in how they entertain themselves.

## My Personal Entertainment Journey

Let me explain how I feel when it comes to entertainment. I am no better than anyone else, but this is where I feel the Lord has led me. I am also trying to lead my home as well. I don't want to allow the Enemy access to my home through entertainment. I feel I have a responsibility to protect myself and my family. God has really done a lot in my life, mainly because I have made it more about Him and less about me. Some people may think it is extreme and a little too much, but I beg to differ. I want to honor Him. I desire to please Him in every way I can.

I was once a huge movie fan. I watched an average of four to five a week. I didn't do any research on movies like I do now either. I watched movies based on who was in them, the amount of violence and action, and how many things were going to be blown up. I did have some standards. I always tried to avoid movies with nudity and a lot of profanity. If it had a small amount of profanity, it really didn't "bother" me as much: I didn't think it was that big of a deal. If it damned God just a little bit, it didn't bother me. That has changed a lot.

If it damns God, I don't watch it. I have "missed" out on watching some "good" movies and it has bothered me less and less. If it has any suggested sexual stuff in it, I don't watch it. If it shows women dressed a certain way a lot, I don't watch it. I do the same with TV shows. I no longer watch one of my favorite reality shows, and some of my favorite TV programs, due to this. I will at times find myself getting entrenched in a TV program, but if it damns God that will be the last time I watch it. I am watching less and less TV now and focusing on things that really matter.

I have decided to protect myself and keep my mind guarded. The result so far? I was struggling in some areas in my life, and I don't anymore. Why? Because I have stopped feeding my flesh, and starved it instead. Therefore, it grows weaker. I enjoyed watching TV and movies. It was a great way to just chill, relax, and spend time with the family. The

## PARENT'S INITIATIVE

problem was that for me to sit down and watch some of these programs or movies was to put my stamp of approval on their content too. I can no longer do that, and I feel stronger spiritually.

I am sometimes with people who mention a movie or TV program they watch and that I had wanted to see, but my research showed that it contained scenes I did not want to see or words I did not want to hear. They'll mention that it was an "awesome movie," but it has this and that in it. They often comment that cursing and sex in movies don't bother them. They think they are so "strong" spiritually that it doesn't bother them. I think that is the wrong question. Does it bother God? To sit there and take part in these things is to say that it's more about you than Him. I know that these sex scenes and cursing bothers God; therefore, it should bother us too. We have somehow convinced ourselves that watching others sin does not affect us, that it has no influence over our hearts and minds. Scripture does not support that idea.

> "A good tree can't produce bad fruit, and a bad tree can't produce good fruit. A tree is identified by its fruit. Figs are never gathered from thornbushes, and grapes are not picked from bramble bushes. A good person produces good things from the treasury of a good heart, and an evil person produces evil things from the treasury of an evil heart. What you say flows from what is in your heart" (Luke 6:43–45).

In our home, we check up on what our kids watch, and we model godly choices ourselves too. A well-known children's program that has been around for many years was talking about the subject of families and how they are broken down. It went on to say that some families have a mommy and daddy, others only have just a mommy or daddy, and then there are those that have two mommies or two daddies. This program was referring to homosexual couples. That was the last time our children watched that show. You may be thinking, *What is the big deal?* If this show is referring to this topic now, it won't long until it addresses the issue of it being okay to be attracted to the same sex. This

# ENTERTAINMENT

is a children's program designed for audiences of a very young age. We must take a stand and set God's standards in our homes.

## Other Forms of Entertainment

We can find different ways to entertain ourselves and our families. When it comes to music and books, take the time to do your research on them. I once read a book that someone recommended. I am embarrassed to even admit this. This person warned me about the language in this book, but I am fascinated by true stories, especially stories about Special Forces in the military. This book had a lot of profanity, but I didn't want to stop reading it because I had spent $13 for it. I regretted it and had to repent for it. It was all about me and the money I had spent.

Music can also play a key influence in the lives of students. Growing up as a teenager, I listened to a lot of music that had some really bad sexual content and a negative message to boot. A lot of the music that students listen to now or that I have heard them talk about is horrible, to the point of embarrassing, when you read the content and what these artist support.

I once took some students on a missions trip to Atlanta. I noticed that one of my students had a key chain of a band that I heard about. I thought it was in his best interest to not wear it because of what they represented. The band had an abbreviation for their name; I asked him if he knew what that meant, and he did. I went on to ask him if his parents knew he had that key chain. Apparently this student's parent bought it for him. That is just another example of a parent being part of the problem and not part of the solution.

When it comes to friends, parents have the responsibility to know with whom their kids are hanging out. I would go as far as to say that parents should know the parents of their student's friends. My kids will not be spending the night at a friend's house if I don't know their parents and what they stand for. If I know they are relaxed in some areas in which they should be strong, my kids won't be staying there. If I have a question about their character, they won't be staying there. Parents can

## PARENT'S INITIATIVE

easily tell by how these other students carry themselves and how they treat others.

We live in a time when you can tell a lot about someone by what they post on social media and by doing some investigating and asking the right questions. What does this have to do with entertainment? It has a lot to do with it, because your kids don't just sit around and do nothing. When they hang out with other people, they are usually finding some form of entertainment. What kind of Internet access will they have with these friends, and what kind of access do these friends have at their home? My son has yet to spend the night at a friend's house, and it may be a long time before we allow that to happen.

As a young teenager I was introduced to porn because of a friend that my parents allowed me to hang out with. He had free access to it at his home, and as a result I struggled with porn for many years of my life. Who is to say that I would not have gotten ahold of it by another means; I will never know. That friendship could have never evolved if my parents would have taken the time to really get to know this individual.

> "Walk with the wise and become wise; associate with fools and get in trouble" (Proverbs 13:20).

### The Worldwide Web

The Internet obviously has its advantages and disadvantages. I use the Internet a lot as a resource, and it truly is a blessing, but it can also be a curse. It blows my mind how so many homes have no accountability when it comes to Internet use. The sad thing is that some children have computers in their rooms and no accountability; they have access to the computer at any time of the day or night. Some computers have filters, but others have no filters whatsoever. That is completely foolish. If young people know what they are doing, they can easily find and get to what they want. Don't be stupid about this. Have some form of accountability when it comes to Internet use in your home.

# ENTERTAINMENT

Put the computer in the living room where everyone can see what's being looked at. Put a password on the computer and spend a little money and buy a filter for it. Know your child's passwords for all their social media and their phones. We are living in a time in which we can have instant access to whatever we want at any time we want. If you have a cell phone with Internet capability, you can access anything. Your children have access to porn on their phones, believe it or not. That's pretty scary to me.

You may be thinking, *Shouldn't they have some kind of privacy?* Really? This is the way I look at it: as long as I am paying for it and they are living under my roof, the only privacy they will get is when they are taking a shower, using the bathroom, or changing their clothes. They are young, naive, and at times very foolish. Their brains are still developing, and they still have problems making the right choices. This is not actually a privacy issue. This has nothing to do with trust. This has everything to do with you being a responsible parent who is strong enough to look out for and take steps to protect the young person you love. The Internet is not a safe place.

We had a situation with one of the girls in our student ministry. Her parents found that she has been chatting with this random guy through a social media site and had shared a lot of information. This guy could have been a sexual predator or stalker—and she had given him her number and address. Her parents were extremely upset about it when they found what was going on. They stripped her of all access to the Internet and her phone. Could this have been avoided? Yes. This is why parents must do their best to be aware of what's going on and who their kids are communicating with in every aspect of their lives.

## Prom, Dances, and Parties! Oh My!

This is where it can really get a little more difficult, but I am just going to take it to the next level. I strongly believe that students should avoid proms and dances until you feel they are mature enough to handle the temptations that they may face. Your student can be a saint, but as a parent it may not be smart to allow them to go.

## PARENT'S INITIATIVE

A lot of bad things can happen at these events. I was one of those guys who knew how to work the crowd there; I knew who was where and what was going on. I got away with some stuff at these events too in spite of the fact that they were "adult supervised" by teachers who really didn't have the guts to deal with students who were doing inappropriate things. Some of these teachers dreaded the fact that they were wasting an evening on watching teenagers dance and have a good time. They didn't want to be there in the first place, so they just met with other teachers and hung out when they were supposed to be supervising.

Events like these open the door for temptations or situations that your student is not ready to face. The music, the touching, the dancing, the thoughts, the provocative way some of the girls dress, the bold way some of the boys act, and many other factors create room for compromise. Times have changed, but there are parents out there who still think they are living in the 1950s when things were different. Don't set up your kids to fail. Protect them. Know all you can about the event and what's going on. Know who is going to be there and do what you can to prepare your kids.

I have heard parents say that they don't want their kids to miss out on the "high school experience." They want their kids to have a good time and be popular and accepted. At what cost? To have their heart broken over and over, to lose their virginity to someone who could care less, to become pregnant, or—even worse—get a sexually transmitted disease (STD) that will haunt them for the rest of their life? There is a price to pay for every decision we make, and especially for every compromise.

One of our former college students attended a Sunday morning church services at our church. This college student was working his way to the seating section where he liked to sit with other students and noticed a girl that he'd seen at a party the other night. He was a little shocked to see her there, but she didn't even notice him. This girl was not even sixteen at the time, but she had been at this party full of college students, doing things that someone her age shouldn't be doing. Why was she there? Did her parents even know?

# ENTERTAINMENT

It all comes down to discretion, parents—doing all you can to find out who is there, who they are hanging out with, meeting parents and knowing what they stand for, and doing all you can to be in the know. You must do all you can to protect and raise your child. It's not about locking them in their rooms and not letting them enjoy their teenage years. It's about helping them make the right choices and setting the standard in your homes. Too many homes are foolishly allowing their children to set the standards for the home. Ultimately this comes down to the "world" setting the standard.

Let me encourage you to not open the door for the Enemy to come into your home and create havoc through how you and your family decide to find entertainment. Do some research and be aware of what is coming in your home through every avenue. Research the content of movies. Find out about the music they are listening to. Check up on your children and keep them accountable. Explain to them the importance of protecting themselves and honoring God in everything they do. Encourage them to also do some research. Teach them to ask the right questions that will lead them to see how important it is for them to protect themselves. Pray with them and encourage them in their walk with the Lord, as you model that to them.

We purged a lot of old DVDs in my house because I no longer wanted that junk in my home. I cleaned out my phone of some secular music that wasn't bad by any means, but I knew these bands were agnostic and have taken their stand in areas with which I do not agree. This is an area you can do something about. It is not about what we give up either. It is about responding from our natural love for Him and pursuing a life of holiness. When it comes to movies, music, the Internet, books, friends, and events, you can do something about it. We can easily close or open these doors. Always think about it this way: Is it more about me and what I want to do? Or is it about Him and what He wants to do through me and my family?

> "Stay alert! Watch out for your great enemy, the devil. He prowls around like a roaring lion, looking for someone

## PARENT'S INITIATIVE

to devour. Stand firm against him, and be strong in your faith. Remember that your family of believers all over the world is going through the same kind of suffering you are" (1 Peter 5:8–9).

## Application Questions for Chapter 9

1. How were you allowed to entertain yourself as a child? Did you allow that to bleed into what you permit now? Are your choices healthy ones?

2. Would God be pleased overall with how you entertain yourself? If not, what personal action steps do you need to take to improve in this area?

3. How do you really feel about your children going to proms, dances, dates, and parties? If you allow them to go to these events, how are you preparing them? If not, what could you do to prepare them?

4. ACTION STEP: Upon evaluation, could you say that there is compromise in your home? In what ways? Music? TV? Internet? Movies? Books? Magazines? Do you think this is affecting your children? Have a family discussion and prayer time about this subject. Make necessary changes.

# Chapter 10: Nonsense and Training

"Repeat them [God's words] again and again to your children. Talk about them when you are at home and when you are on the road, when you are going to bed and when you are getting up. Tie them to your hands and wear them on your forehead as reminders. Write them on the doorposts of your house and on your gates" (Deuteronomy 6:7–9).

Raising kids is not as easy as some parents make it out to be. Some parents make it seem really easy, and it makes most people sick to their stomachs. You may be wondering, *What am I doing wrong?* when you sit back and look at other parents and how their kids act. Their behavior makes some newlywed couples think twice about having kids in the first place. Think about those times when that cute kid you saw in the grocery aisle suddenly morphed into this screaming and foaming-out-of-the-mouth little monster throwing a temper tantrum at the checkout line. Usually this happens because they saw something they wanted and could not get it. You've got to admit, the marketing plan was clever: Who decided to line up all the candy at the checkout register? I wish I could meet this person and give him a piece of my mind.

I have seen some funny and embarrassing situations for parents. I have even seen teenagers who definitely should know better show total disrespect for their parents in front of everyone. Those parents just smiled, turned red in the face, and said that kids will be kids.

## PARENT'S INITIATIVE

For the past couple of years, our church has done a back-to-school outreach. We get some groceries together, some school clothes, school supplies, and backpacks, and people from the community come to our church, where we hand these items out. This one particular year, we decided to cook hot dogs and hand them out as families left. We had a volunteer come to help up with her kids, but these kids were not the kind you left unattended. What was shocking was that their second oldest was the biggest problem and made the biggest scene.

We decided that we were not going to give our volunteers hot dogs until after the event because we wanted to make sure we had enough for those who came to be served at the outreach. I thought this was a great idea: it would be embarrassing to run out of hot dogs. A twelve-year-old student threw a serious temper tantrum because we told him he couldn't get a hot dog until after the outreach. I am not kidding! He was at the point of crying and throwing himself on the floor. He literally fell butt-first on a chair, cried loudly, and threw his face on his hands to cover his eyes. These were not even all-beef hot dogs! His mom didn't do anything about it either. She was actually upset at us because we didn't give him one. There are some of you sitting there and wondering, *Why didn't you just give him a hot dog and be done with it?* That is the problem. A twelve-year-old shouldn't be acting like that; nor should a five-year-old. That is nonsense.

Nonsense can be seen as an idea, possibly a behavior, or even some kind of statement that is not true or just doesn't make sense at all. Nonsense is something that I have dealt with on many levels, from babies, kids, and teenagers to young adults and even senior citizens. Yes, senior citizens.

I was once invited to a birthday party by a former student. She had one of those mini motorized motorcycles. There were a lot of us there, and we were all having a great time taking turns and riding it in the backyard of her house. This was a little surprising to me. They were all civilized and not fighting over who was next. Then my turn came, and they were all getting a kick out of a five foot eleven and close to two hundred and seventy-pound (at the time) student pastor riding this

## NONSENSE AND TRAINING

minibike. They were laughing, but I didn't care because I was having fun. Then along came her little brother. He was probably about ten. He also wanted to ride it. (Let me remind you that he owned the bike. He could ride it any time, especially after his sister's birthday party.) When he showed up, everything became focused on him. Forget that this was his sister's birthday party; it was all about him. He started crying and throwing a temper tantrum because he had to wait his turn. When it came to his turn, he didn't want to get off and refused to do so. His dad just stood there, laughing and turning beet red. The crazy thing was that as others were riding before his turn, the kid tried to push them off and even tried to put an object in the wheel to get them thrown off the bike. That is nonsense!

It would have been so much better if the parents had dealt with the nonsense, especially if they had begun when their child was at a young age, not waiting until it was too late. That twelve-year-old wanting a hot dog and throwing a fit because we didn't give him one was total nonsense. That ten-year-old who did not know how to share with others and tried to hurt others, whose dad just stood there and laughed about it because he was too embarrassed to deal with it. That was also nonsense.

I can share more nonsense stories. Nonsense is just that: nonsense! To me, nonsense can be a lot of things. I am sure you can also come up with other means of nonsense and even share some great stories. There may be stories of times that you may have witnessed some drama with your own eyes at a store or even a family gathering. You may even be able to think of stories that occurred in your very own house. I would just like to be a fly on the wall in the house of that twelve- or ten-year-old. If they acted like that in public, just imagine how bad it must be in their home.

Nonsense needs to be dealt with, and God has given us the tools to deal with it. We do our kids an injustice when we don't deal with it and allow nonsense to slide. I am around teenagers all the time, and they know that my wife and I don't put up with nonsense. I once took fourteen students to a camp all by myself. I didn't have one bad thing

## PARENT'S INITIATIVE

happen. I was a student pastor for over thirteen years, and I have never had anything "serious" happen (knock on wood).

Before we took any trip or did an event, I would give them the "speech" and they knew I was serious. I put the fear of God into them. They knew that we deal with things swiftly and if it came down to it, it would be the last event they went on for a long time. It might even be the last event they went on as long as I was there.

There is no reason for me to put up with nonsense or allow other students' experiences to be messed up because of someone else's nonsense. The sad thing is that I have seen students be more respectful towards my wife, myself, and our leaders than they are to their own parents. It's because we have chosen not to put up with it and are very good at holding them accountable. I am sure we have lost some students because of it. That's OK. There has to be a standard. I have a responsibility and I don't need to waver from it.

> "Train up a child in the way he should go: and when he is old, he will not depart from it" (Proverbs 22:6 KJV).

When it comes to dealing with nonsense, I think it's safe to say that you will not have to deal with it as often when there is some good training going on. To give effective training is to educate, give instruction to, or to discipline the person or thing that is being trained.

When you are educating your child on how they should act, they will learn and grow from it. In a perfect world, they will learn the first time you sit down and try explaining to them what the deal is, but we all know that usually isn't the case. Consistent discipline needs to come into play. It is critical that we realize that as parents, we need to be consistent and always make the necessary changes.

Let's go back to Proverbs 22:6. I read a very good explanation of this Scripture. Paraphrased, it said that truly raising and training a child within the context of this proverb begins with the Bible. Second Timothy 3:16 talks about how the Bible is God-breathed and is useful for teaching, rebuking, correcting, and training. In 2 Timothy 3:15, you

## NONSENSE AND TRAINING

see that Scripture taught from a young age will grant important truths on salvation; 2 Timothy 3:17 talks about how it prepares us to do every good work. First Peter 3:15 stresses that we must always put God first and be prepared to share our testimony. So it's safe to say that we as parents need to do our part in implementing the Word in our kids.

> "Children are a gift from the Lord; they are a reward from him" (Psalm 127:3).

Some of you may be thinking that there is no way that this is found in the Bible. Go ahead and look it up! God blessed you with your child, but it's up to you as a parent to do your part. The questions that need to asked are: *Have you been a good steward of the gift God has given you? Have you been raising your children in a manner that pleases the Lord?*

If you do an in-depth study of this Scripture, you will see why they are a gift. There are two reasons: 1) God has entrusted you with them to further build His kingdom and 2) to extend your family legacy. When you factor that there are people in this world who can't bear children and are paying a lot of money to, many times, only fail time and time again, you must realize that He blessed you with your child. That is a gift.

In order for us to further build His kingdom and extend a great legacy, the Word has to be the cornerstone of our roles as parents. Moses stressed the importance of implementing the Word in Deuteronomy 6:7–9, so much so that it needs to be visible everywhere. He would go on to say that obedience to the Word of God will help you "live safely in the land" (Leviticus 25:18 NIV), that all will "go well" with you (Deuteronomy 12:28 NIV), and that God will bless you in the land that you occupy (Deuteronomy 30:16).

Scripture stresses to all parents alike that the Word of God is the basis of raising and training a child to know God and to live the life they are called to live. Knowing God and the Word is what will draw them to God for salvation. It will also teach them what sin is and how to deal with that sin. Every young child can get ahold of this and understand the need for forgiveness at a very young age. We saw this in our son Zane.

## PARENT'S INITIATIVE

We try our best to be consistent with him, and we also try our best to sit down and explain to him why we do what we do and what the Word says. At a very young age he was asking questions about God and His forgiveness. He is still asking questions and trying to wrap his small mind around God, and my wife and I have realized the importance of being the best representation of God we can be for our son. We are extending the best example that we can set for love, mercy, and grace, but also giving discipline when it is necessary.

Discipline is the most important part of raising godly children. The Bible talks about how the Lord disciplines those that He loves (Proverbs 3:12). We should never take discipline lightly or be bothered by it because the Bible also talks about how God disciplines those that He considers as sons (Hebrews 12:5–6). We are disciplined so that we can share in the holiness of God (Hebrews 12:10). So, when we discipline our children, they will receive wisdom. It is also important to not delay when discipline is necessary.

> "When people have a dispute, they are to take it to court and the judges will decide the case, acquitting the innocent and condemning the guilty. If the guilty person deserves to be beaten, the judge shall make them lie down and have them flogged in his presence with the number of lashes the crime deserves, but the judge must not impose more than forty lashes. If the guilty party is flogged more than that, your fellow Israelite will be degraded in your eyes" (Deuteronomy 5:1–3 NIV).

What does this have to do with parenting? This actually has a lot to do with it because you learn a couple of things here when it comes to effective discipline. It's not the flogging part, even though there may come a time when it seems a flogging may be necessary according to what your children may have been done. What I like here is how swiftly discipline was taken. When we are responsible for others, there are times when discipline has to be administered—whether it is for your own child, a student, or even an employee.

## NONSENSE AND TRAINING

Obviously we approach discipline differently for each occasion or relationship, but there are three things you can take from this example and administer when discipline is necessary. 1) Punishment should take place not too long after the individual does something that needs discipline. 2) The degree of the punishment should reflect the seriousness of what took place. 3) Don't overdo the punishment. When discipline is handled quickly, justly, and with restraint, it makes its point while also saving the dignity of the person deserving punishment. Think things though. It may help to take a couple of deep breaths.

> "To discipline a child produces wisdom, but a mother is disgraced by an undisciplined child" (Proverbs 29:15).

Isn't that spot-on and the truth? It reminds me of the earlier story about the kids at the store. The Bible also goes on to tell us that a disciplined child will bring us peace and respect (Hebrews 12:9).

> "Discipline your children, and they will give you peace of mind and will make your heart glad" (Proverbs 29:17).

As a matter of fact, children want discipline because it is a sign of love. That is why those kids that grow up in homes with no discipline feel unloved and are more likely to grow up disobeying those in authority as they grow older. Some of you may disagree with me, but there really isn't much of an argument because of what the Word of God says.

I am a firm believer in spanking my children as a form of discipline. Do I do it every time? No. I do it when I think it's really necessary. My wife and I speak first and then take action. At times we offer a warning, or possibly two warnings, first. We take action when we must. We are not abusive. There is a difference. My wife has told my son multiple times that the Lord has given him extra padding on his butt so that he could be spanked. Nor do we believe in embarrassing our kids. Spanking should be done privately. We have almost mastered something that all parents should work on and that's the "chill before the wrath comes."

## PARENT'S INITIATIVE

It's the part in which you take a few moments before you spank your children and calm down. I believe the worst thing you can do is unleash your wrath at that moment, because it will be worse. Take a few moments and collect yourself. We don't use our hands to spank our kids, nor do we use a belt. I am sure that some of you who were spanked as a child with either of these items still flinch when you see a belt or when a hand is raised at you. I catch myself ducking or even about to run at times. My parents used whatever was at the ready. Whether it was a metal spoon, a broomstick, a belt, their hand, a washrag, or a twig, it was used to spank me and my sister. This may sound foolish, but my wife and I used a wooden spoon on my son when he was younger. It is now being used on our daughter; my son has been upgraded to a paddle. The spoon was recommended and it worked. The paddle was something we came up with on our own. The last time I got spanked at school was with a plastic paddle, so I assumed if it was "safe" enough to be used at school, I could use it on my own kids. Where does it say it in the Bible that we should spank our kids?

> "Those who spare the rod of discipline hate their children. Those who love their children care enough to discipline them" (Proverbs 13:24).
>
> "A youngster's heart is filled with foolishness, but physical discipline will drive it far away" (Proverbs 22:15).
>
> "Don't fail to discipline your children. The rod of punishment won't kill them. Physical discipline may well save them from death" (Proverbs 23:13–14).

Even though my parents were a little extreme at times, I believe I am who I am today because of the discipline that was instilled in me. There are times my mom has apologized to me because they were so hard on me, but I thank her for it. I have learned from them, the good and the negative, and have used the good on my own kids. It's not easy to discipline my kids, by any means. I find no pleasure in it, but I know

## NONSENSE AND TRAINING

what the Bible says I must do and I know that it will help in shaping and forming my kids. I don't spank them for every little mistake, but I do it when it's necessary. We also use other forms of discipline, whether it's taking something away from them or even making them do something they hate doing.

My son hates staying still at times, and we have made him sit in a corner and just look at the wall. That drove him crazy because he is so active. We had our daughter write a hundred sentences because of something she did once, and you would've thought it was the end of the world.

> "No discipline is enjoyable while it is happening—it's painful! But afterward there will be a peaceful harvest of right living for those who are trained in this way" (Hebrews 12:11).

Parents ask us about our kids a lot. Trust me. Our kids aren't perfect. I am very proud to say that for the most part they are well-behaved. They may act foolish sometimes, but not as much as other kids I have been around. The key is consistency! Follow up at all times and don't let things slide. You must allow room for grace and mercy, and allow them to make mistakes, but be sure they learn from them. Sit down and talk with them. Learn to ask the right questions and allow them to see the reasoning behind it all.

Some folks may think that this is a little too much, but every time we discipline our kids, we sit down and talk to them about it afterward. We wait till they have calmed down and our blood pressure is down, and then we talk. We want them to understand why we disciplined them and that we love them. We also hug them and pray for them afterwards.

> "Fathers, do not provoke your children to anger by the way you treat them. Rather, bring them up with the discipline and instruction that comes from the Lord" (Ephesians 6:4).

## PARENT'S INITIATIVE

Just as it is important to find a balance in being too passive or aggressive, a balance has to be found in dealing with nonsense and training (discipline). The word "fathers" in Ephesians 6:4 could be translated as parents which includes the mother as well. During this time period, it was mainly the father who handled discipline. The mother had a hand in enforcing things, but it was up to the father to set things straight and see that their kids were raised in the way God intended. Many dads today have an attitude that is not honoring the interaction God intended they have in raising and disciplining their children. They have the mentality that they are making the money, so it is the responsibility of the mother to raise the kids. This is not the instruction the Bible gives. The direction of the home came down from the father.

Parents need to make sure they are on the same page when it comes to disciplining their children, and fathers need to make sure they are also playing a role in this area. The key in this Scripture is that parents don't provoke their kids in such a way that they completely lose control and break out against authority. When discipline is implemented to the point of being overboard, it will push kids in a direction that will cause them to rebel. There has to be correction and training. There has to be grace and forgiveness extended. There has to be some understanding and love implemented; if not, it will drive your kids away.

I know of two students whose parents are divorced. These students really don't want much to do with their father because he has become too much. They would rather stay with their mother. It's not because she lets them get away with everything; it's because the father is so overbearing and always getting on their case. In many ways, this father is expecting more from them than they are ready to give.

Then there is the other extreme: parents who haven't found a balance and don't want to be too harsh (maybe because it was too much for them growing up), so they decide not to discipline at all. When there is a lack of discipline in a home, it will make a child insecure, miserable, and self-centered. These children are allowed to make decisions on their own that they have no business making on

## NONSENSE AND TRAINING

their own. This causes a problem because they don't have the mental capacity to make their own decisions. Parents should be making some of these decisions for their kids and helping them avoid some of the same mistakes they made.

As a child grows up over time, physical discipline will be replaced with more communication and encouragement, as well as helping your kids with more guidance. It needs to be shown in love and with some sternness when needed. It doesn't mean that we relax and let things slide. It just means that parents may use a different means of enforcing things. I have read that the best time to use a physical means of punishment should be reserved between the ages of eighteen months and ten years.

While I was a teenager, my mom reached a point when she realized that physical discipline was no longer going to work on me. I was about sixteen and almost two times bigger than she was. I was playing football and lifting weights all the time. She tried to discipline me, and I didn't budge at all. That is when she changed her methods. She began to take away things, and that hurt me more than physical discipline. She changed her method, and it got my attention.

Parents need to be passionate about raising their kids. I know it may seem hard at times, and you may wish you could have a do-over or even exchange your kids. Remember that they were given to you as a reward and that we need to be good stewards of what God has blessed us with. We have a short time with our kids; during that time, we are responsible for dealing with nonsense and training (raising them in the ways of the Lord). Reflect on the promise of Proverbs: it says that when a child is diligently trained in the way they should go, they will have a hard time departing from it. (See Proverbs 22:6.) Be consistent and don't give up. Your training will always be with them, and it will be hard for them to ignore it. Implement the Word as much as you can and take one day at a time. It is never too late. Be sure to continue to trust in the Lord for direction and guidance and study the Word.

# PARENT'S INITIATIVE

## Application Questions for Chapter 10

1. What are some things that would fall into the "nonsense" category? How are you dealing with it? Is the manner you are dealing with it effective? If not, what could you do differently?

2. Were you disciplined as a child? Was it done correctly or incorrectly? Are you implementing it in the same way? Are there things you need to avoid?

3. Do you find yourself holding back because of your past, and has that affected your family in a bad way? Were you possibly not disciplined as you needed to be, leading to you following the same example?

4. Would you be guilty of being too aggressive when it comes to discipline? If so, what action steps can you take to avoid that?

5. ACTION STEP: Read Psalm 119:9–16. The Word of God is a treasure that is stored up within our hearts. Brainstorm ways you can instill the Word in your family together. Make a plan to try some of the ideas you came up with.

# Chapter 11: Sex

"God's will is for you to be holy, so stay away from all sexual sin. Then each of you will control his own body and live in holiness and honor—not in lustful passion like the pagans who do not know God and his ways" (1 Thessalonians 4:35).

You may be wondering what sex has to do with parenting. It has a lot more to do with parenting than you think. I learned about sex at a very young age and wasn't even aware of the fact that I wasn't supposed to be touched in certain ways. As a young child I was molested several times by a couple of different people, people who my parents trusted to watch me, but my parents had no clue what was going on. I had no clue what was really going on either; I thought it was OK because I was told by these individuals that it was OK. I was told that it was natural. This began around the time I was five and continued until I was about eight.

Around the age of twelve or thirteen, I was introduced to sex with the opposite sex when a friend brought a pornographic videotape to my house. We watched it as if we were just watching a movie. That was when the addiction to pornography began in my life and I struggled with it for many years. During my high school years, I had access to porn all the time: at home, through the Internet, friends lending me movies or magazines; and when I was old enough, I went to great lengths to purchase it. When you really want something bad enough, you will do what is necessary to get it. My mom found my stash a couple of times,

## PARENT'S INITIATIVE

but that really didn't stop me. I would just get more and find another hiding place.

I was allowed to date, and I dated several girls as a teenager. Looking back on it now, I am not proud of that. I had no accountability in dating these girls. There was one girl in particular who I dated for a long period of time. The crazy thing is that her parents allowed us to be alone in her room with the door closed! I was allowed to spend the night several times at their house, in the bedroom right next to hers, too. We didn't "officially" have sex but we came close to it several times. We were also allowed to go on dates by ourselves. With another girl, I went to her house in the middle of the night several times and we "fooled" around.

I was allowed to go to dances, proms, and parties, and there was little supervision present at these events. If it was crazy back then in the late '90s, I can only imagine how bad it is now. The way we danced back then was very inappropriate, and I know that it has become worse. I remember the thoughts that went through my mind as a teenager while I was dancing with those girls. I was touching them inappropriately while I danced with them. The way the guys talked about these girls before, during, and after these events would make any father want to kill someone.

I don't share all that information to boast about my bad past, by any means. I don't share those thoughts to jar you back to a time that maybe you have chosen to forget either. I mentioned these things to make parents aware of the importance of talking about sex with their children—not just when they reach a certain age and you sit down and have the "birds and bees" talk. It has to be done on a regular basis, and there has to be accountability. A lot of the things that I mentioned could be taking place in your home, and you have no idea. Your child could be molested and think it is okay. Your child could be addicted to porn, and you might have no clue. Your child could be going out on dates and having sex, and you do not know about it. Your child could seem trustworthy but be playing you like a fool.

I honestly don't remember having "the talk" with my parents. I do remember when my mom found my stash of porn a couple of times and

# SEX

came into my room. She really didn't say much, but I knew she was disgusted. That didn't stop me from getting more though. For a time there, I did not think there was anything wrong with what I was doing. I thought it was natural. I thought all guys looked at porn. I am pretty sure my parents didn't get "the talk" either. There are a lot of parents out there who are embarrassed by it. That is one of the biggest mistakes a parent can make.

My wife and I were recently discussing how we needed to have "the talk" with our son. He was at that age when he was beginning to ask a lot of questions. To be honest, I was dreading it. I knew it had to be done, because I did not want him to go through what I went through. In the time we are living in, I wanted him to have "the talk" with us rather than someone else. My wife asked our pastor about doing this. They discussed it for a bit and he gave her a book. This book discussed and showed us the importance of talking to our kids about sex and how they came into this world.

It is actually a book series that is a great tool in helping parents talk to their kids about sex, beginning at the age of three. (Yes, you read that correctly. Three is the age at which this series begins.) Called *God's Design for Sex* by Stan and Brenna Jones, the series is broken down into four different stages. Parents are encouraged to sit down with their kids at different ages and read these books to them. Doing this engenders a discussion.

When I first saw these books I was a little shocked by some of the pictures, but they really made a lot of sense. I had not learned some of this stuff until health class in ninth grade! The more I thought about it, the more relieved I became. I would rather have our kids sit down and see this firsthand with us than sit down with someone else, or in a school for that matter, and get it wrong.

My wife sat down with my son and read two books from this series because he had some catching up to do. He was a little behind in the series, but this allowed for some open discussion. They talked about some things and then he proceeded to tell her that some of the kids had already begun to talk about sex and some of the things mentioned in the

## PARENT'S INITIATIVE

book at his school. He is only going into the second grade! To think the fact that seven- to eight-year-olds are already discussing sex is pretty scary. So much has changed since I was a teenager. As each day goes by, it is only getting worse. Some parents get it, while others don't.

We were able to begin with my daughter when she turned three, and I am so glad that we could do that. I will never forget the day she came home from school as a kindergartner and informed us about what happened in PE class that day. Out of nowhere, she said that two girls had gotten in trouble that day. My wife asked her why, and she replied that they were performing a wedding ceremony with one another. We are talking about two little girls exchanging wedding vows with one another! It's very possible that it was done innocently, but my daughter knew that it wasn't good for them to do that because we sat down and talked about it.

The access that our students have to sexual material is a lot easier than it used to be when I was teenager. I am sure that some parents aren't aware that students can access porn on their smartphones, tablets, and even gaming devices. My son has a handheld game system. My wife set it up so he cannot access the Internet on it. If our children have access to the Internet on any device, they can have access to porn. Books and magazines are just as bad. There are magazines (geared to young girls) that tell them how they can have the best sex ever. Books today give very vivid descriptions of sexual situations, which in turn arouses that desire in our students. TV programs and movies depict that it is okay to have sex before marriage and that it is okay to have multiple partners on top of that.

Music talks about sex in detail. Kids are dancing to it and thinking about the things it suggests—things they shouldn't be thinking about. There are kids who are allowed to have a TV with cable access in their rooms with no safeguards set for them. They can watch anything they want. There are also those students who are given a computer with Internet access and no accountability. This is foolish.

Schools are handing out condoms and telling kids that if they have sex, to be sure to have safe sex. Some parents do this too. Truthfully,

# SEX

safe sex outside of marriage does not exist. The best thing that students can do is not have sex until they get married. Parents need to push the importance of waiting instead of encouraging their children to flow along with the culture we live in. God designed sex to be between a husband and wife. I am sure there are some parents who are not aware of the fact that one out of three sexually active people have a sexually transmitted disease and are not even aware of it. An STD can lay dormant for up to six years.

Today girls are put on birth control to help regulate their menstrual cycles at an early age sometimes, but their parents are opening an avenue for temptation for them in doing this. Some of these pills can cause some serious complications in the future if parents don't do their research. We know of a young girl who recently was prescribed birth control pills to help regulate her menstrual cycle. This has been known to cause sterility in some women. Another girl we know was put on birth control pills and became pregnant shortly after. Yet another became sexually active, and her parents were too naive to believe she was having sex on a regular basis; in fact, she has had multiple partners at a very young age. Please don't get me wrong: I totally understand medical reasons. Just be sure to check into every avenue before possibly setting up your child for failure.

Parents are setting up their kids to fail all the time when it comes to sex. A lot of this failure stems from a lack of accountability or just being too passive because they are too lazy to talk about it. Most parents can see there may be a problem with the way their kids talk about or even treat the opposite sex. There are also those cases in which there may be an attraction to the same sex.

Parents have to go beyond their own embarrassment and possible shame over this subject because of their own mistakes in the past. It is a topic that some older students could easily throw back in the face of their parents, but that should not stop you as a parent. Truly you do not want them to make the same mistakes you made anyway. We have a responsibility and a gift that God has blessed us with. Talking to your kids about sex is being a good steward: you are raising your kids to the standard of purity that God desires.

## PARENT'S INITIATIVE

This book is all about being aware as a parent; it is also about being aware of what the Bible has to say in these areas. It's up to parents to make the right choices and apply what they learn and what they are taught. I am not trying to give you the answers. As I mentioned earlier, in many cases the awareness and know-how is there, but nothing is being done about it. That is how parents are part of the problem and are not offering a solution.

If I could offer one suggestion on how to protect your kids in the sex department, it would be to not allow your kids to date, to not allow your kids to have boyfriends or girlfriends. It blows my mind how parents are pushing their kids to do this at a very young age. They are even teasing them with it as little kids.

> "Promise me, O women of Jerusalem, not to awaken love until the time is right" (Song of Solomon 8:4).

To push your kids to date, or even encourage it, will awaken love before the time is right. One of the things that I have said to our students on several different occasions is that they will not be capable of truly loving someone the way that God intended until they love God first. Think about that statement. It is the truth. It is hard to really love anyone else until you love God the way you were intended to do. I was not fully capable of loving my wife the way I needed until I loved God in the way I needed. When we start to understand His love, it is easier to forgive, to extend grace, to show mercy, and even to love when it is difficult to love. I do not think we can grasp how much God loves us because His love is so perfect, but we get a concept of it from knowing Him. His love helps us to understand how to love someone else.

Teenagers or even young adults are very capable of loving someone. I am not saying that they can't; but if they are not mature enough to handle it, it can lead to some bad situations and build a pile of regret for their future. As I stated before, most students are not capable of making their own decisions on a regular basis. So, how can they be capable

# SEX

of truly loving someone else of the opposite sex and be romantically involved?

I was watching a TV program that involved victims of sexual crimes. It referred to cases that had actually happened but added a little drama to them. This one episode was about pedophiles and how they prey on young children. A young woman took the stand in a court of law on the show and was a witness for the defendant. She had had a sexual relationship with this thirty-year-old guy from the time she was eleven until she was fourteen! She was infatuated with this guy. At the time, she was being molested; she was also being physically abused by her father, and her mother was a drunk. This guy was her neighbor and knew how to pick his victims. This young girl was vulnerable, and the guy took advantage of it.

I know this is just a TV program, but there are many cases like this in real life. This girl was still actually in love with the guy and he continued to take advantage of her. She was defending him as a pedophile. The only reason he left her was because she had hit puberty and he didn't care for her any longer. She was blinded to the fact that he had taken advantage of her—just like a lot of our young ladies and guys today.

Growing up, I knew how to work the system when it came to dating other girls, just as many students do today. They have definitely become more smooth and craftier than I was. If a parent is foolish enough to leave their kids alone with the opposite sex, they are asking for trouble. Your kids can be the greatest kids in the world and very trustworthy. You might be able to trust them with your life, but there is no way you can trust what is between their legs.

If you are going to allow your kids to date, at least be smart about it. Don't set them up for failure. Don't leave them alone at any time; even driving in a car alone can set them up for failure. Going to a party can set them up for failure. Not knowing the parents of the student that your child is dating and how they feel about these things, or not knowing the standards they have set, can set your kids up for failure. You will be better off as a parent to not allow it and encourage your student to wait.

## PARENT'S INITIATIVE

If you're willing to allow this to happen, then prepare them for it. Walk through different scenarios with them and help them form an action plan. You can't keep them locked away forever, so prepare them for the future. Just don't send them out when they are not ready!

There has been a growing trend among many Christian families to help their children find mates through the groups in which they already participate. Many kids today go on group dates of sorts. Guys and girls may be interested in one another, but the focus is first on becoming friends. These are chaperoned situations. If a young man becomes seriously interested in a young woman, he goes to her parents and speaks to them about how to court her. More and more families are handling this time in their children's lives in this manner. It keeps their children safe and gives them real time to get to know each other.

Even after they begin to court, a young couple is supervised. The intention is to get married from the beginning so that your children are not learning to make and break relationships. The young couple does not go anywhere alone and does not show physical affection. The only form of physical touch is a side hug. Many save their first kiss for their wedding day. These families do feel countercultural in today's society, but they are very serious about their choices. These parents are tired of seeing young people's lives being destroyed and have decided that they will do all they can to not let that happen to their own. They know their children must make their own decisions in the end, but they are committed to outfitting them with all the tools they need to do it. They have found good communication to be their most powerful tool. When children know that their parents are listening to them and care about them, they also know they are not fighting their battles alone. Young women and young men are taught about purity of heart in every aspect of their lives from the ground up. Some parents and grown-up children of this generation have even written books on the subject to encourage the ones coming up.

When a young couple begins to court, they must interact with both of their families on a regular basis. This brings about even more accountability and highlights the seriousness of the commitment. The

# SEX

focus of the relationship is less emotional and, obviously, less physical as well. Doing this sets a standard and protects the couple's purity in many ways, but it also allows other, more practical issues to emerge: How well do they get along? What kinds of things do they still need to learn? What kind of timeline is best for them? How will they support themselves when married? What kinds of callings are on their lives? All of these questions are ahead of them, and some of them will come into play now—before they are married. The discussions they have now can change their lives.

I want to stress that there is absolutely nothing wrong with students "liking" one another. That is going to happen and that is natural. You may trust your student enough to go out in "group settings." If that's the case for you, then so be it. Once again, accountability is vital, and knowing who is going to be there and where they are going is important. Sometimes fighting against something will only cause more of a problem or even increase attraction. A group setting with which you are at peace is the best way for others to truly get to know one another.

Once again, talk to your kids about sex. Begin at an early age. Hold them accountable and don't let them make the same mistakes you made (if you made any). Set up safeguards in your home. Know your kid's friends and their parents, especially when they are going to their house all the time. I recently scheduled an appointment with a student to sit down and just talk. I noticed that this student was going in the wrong direction and was concerned for her. I sat down with her for about two hours and I couldn't believe what was said had recently taken place. She confessed that she had recently lost her virginity. She had lied to her parents about going to someone else's house, saying their parents would be there as well. Not one time did the two sets of parents meet, but they willingly allowed them to go on dates and be alone. This student's parents had been under the teaching of our church for a long time and this still took place. I was flabbergasted.

I once preached on the story of Samson and Delilah in our student ministry. A few days before I spoke, I was mowing my lawn and praying/thinking about the message I was about to give. Then, like a light going

## PARENT'S INITIATIVE

off in my head, I realized what was really taking place in the life of Samson: he was guilty of "prostituting" his heart away. He was giving something away that really didn't belong to him. It belonged to God first. He was constantly giving his heart away to other girls and not making the Lord his number one. This is the very thing a lot of students are guilty of day in and day out. Not just students, but adults as well.

Really think about it for a second. We sell out our hearts for things that are not really worth it, and we do it over and over again. We end up giving God leftovers. We give our heart away, take it back, give it away, take it back; and it becomes this endless cycle. Students and adults alike do it with relationships, possessions, priorities, and so on. When our heart first belongs to God, then everything else falls in its proper place. If God is not first, we are giving something that doesn't belong to us in the first place. Parents need to instill in their kids the importance of putting the Lord first! We must model giving our hearts completely to God first; everything else will follow, as it should, to the last.

We have yet to let our son spend the night at a friend's house, and we do not allow him to visit other people's houses unless we have a close relationship with the parents. People may think that I am a little too protective. I don't think I am at all. I am not living in denial. I see the direction this world is going in and how so many people have compromised in many ways. I don't want to set my kids up to fail because they have yet to fully understand compromise themselves. My son will come home from school, or even church, at times and talk about what his friends are allowed to do, and it blows my mind. It's just confirmation for the way I feel, and I add another name to the checklist of homes he will not stay in. It is sad that parents allow their children to watch programs and movies that will hurt their minds and hearts. It is wrong that parents give their children unlimited and unfiltered access to the Internet. Be smart and do some research. Sit down with your kids and have "the talk" on a frequent basis.

I do not have all the answers, but I want to raise awareness in your home. Many young people are failing and struggling in an area that they shouldn't be dealing with at all at such a young age. It is the parents who

# SEX

have opened the door and pushed their kids through it. No safeguards have been set, and they are awakening an area in their child's life that the child is not mature enough to handle. That should not be.

Accountability is vital, and to be in the know is also important. Keep your eyes and ears open and be in the loop. Know what's going on and what's coming up. As a parent, it's your responsibility to care for your child and to know what is happening in their hearts and minds. God gave them to you. Take care of them.

## Application Questions for Chapter 11

1. Have you avoided the sex talk with your children? If so, why? Will you commit to having that talk?
2. Are you doing your best to keep your kids accountable? If not, what do you think you need to do?
3. Have you allowed your child's "love" to be awakened before it is time? If so, what can you do to bring it down a notch?
4. Do you and your children communicate well? How can you make that better?
5. ACTION STEP: What safeguards have you placed in your children's lives? If you haven't, what needs to be done? Do it.

# Chapter 12: Neglecting Awareness

*"But don't just listen to God's word. You must do what it says. Otherwise, you are only fooling yourselves"*
*(James 1:22).*

Once we are made aware of something, we have the responsibility to do something about it. Too often, people see something that needs to change in their own lives and do nothing. They are either too lazy to put forth the effort to bring change or they are content with their current situation. Then when they reach a breaking point, it is often a little too late to make the needed changes. Many times, God is the One who makes us aware of the changes we need to be make; other times, we just naturally realize that a change needs to take place. A majority of addicts are aware that they have an addiction and still choose to do nothing about it. There are many, many places that offer free help to overcome those addictions, yet they choose to neglect the help they could receive.

This happens in the church too. Christians often find themselves struggling. I have, myself. God makes us aware of something that we need to change, and we neglect it. We push it to the side, thinking that maybe we will deal with it later. However, God is telling us that now is the time. He knows it will be more difficult to deal with it later. Or, possibly, later will be too late. We say we want God to do something in our lives and take us to new heights. We say we want a deeper relationship with Him, but often have not yet begun to work on the things that He has

## PARENT'S INITIATIVE

already shown us! God is probably not going to move on your behalf until you obey Him in the things He has already spoken to you about. Change has to take place.

God sent the Holy Spirit to bring this awareness to us. He was sent to speak into our lives and give us guidance. He was sent as an advocate on behalf of God and Jesus Christ, which means He was sent to speak on their behalf! He is there to bring us truth and help us avoid any trouble that we might bring upon ourselves.

> "But the Advocate, the Holy Spirit, whom the Father will send in my name, will teach you all things and will remind you of everything I have said to you" (John 14:26 NIV).

Jesus was speaking to His disciples, promising them that the Holy Spirit would remind them of everything they had been taught. They had witnessed with their own eyes the miracles that had taken place and heard amazing messages that would always stay with them. Just as the Holy Spirit was promised to them, He was also promised to us. Through the Holy Spirit, we are reminded of the things that we have read and studied in the Bible and have heard in church or Bible studies that we have attended.

It's crazy to think so many people are struggling in their own lives and homes when they have been given the tools to succeed. We have been given the Bible, which is the Word of God (inspired by God Himself), the Holy Spirit, the church, and other believers who God has strategically placed in our lives to help us in times of need and struggle. Yet we still choose to neglect the awareness that we have been given at times. Let me remind you once again that I am guilty of this as well. We have been given freedom, and we choose to neglect it.

> "For the Lord is the Spirit, and wherever the Spirit of the Lord is, there is freedom" (2 Corinthians 3:17).

# NEGLECTING AWARENESS

I want freedom in my life and I want freedom in my home. I don't want to bring bondage in my life or my home because I have neglected the awareness that God has brought into my life. As parents, we have this huge responsibility to deal with things that we see in our children. We know it is vital to not only deal with what's going on in our own spiritual lives but also in our homes. Our homes will not go beyond the spiritual level that has been set by the parents. If we continue to neglect the truth God gives us, we had better prepare for turmoil and conflict in our homes.

Most of you have already begun to see some things and are taking the initiative to make some necessary changes. Others are just sitting back and doing nothing. To pray and hope it will fix itself without doing anything, my friend, is insanity. You are doing the same thing over and over again and expecting different results. That is the same as doing nothing. This idea applies to our own personal lives and our homes too. We say we want God to be the center of our lives and in our homes; but in our choices, we push Him to the side. We neglect the truth and awareness, the advice, and the reminders He gives, and yet we expect things to change for the better in our lives and homes.

I want to share a couple of stories found in the Bible of fathers who were made aware of things that were taking place in the lives of their children and their households but didn't do anything about it. I pray that these stories will show you the seriousness of being made aware of things and neglecting to take action. These stories not only show us what can and what will happen when action is not taken: they also serve as a reminder of why we should listen and take action when the Holy Spirit shows us things in our own lives and in our homes as parents.

## Eli and His Sons

The story of Eli and his sons illustrates the setting in many homes. This is a great example of a father who has worked hard to build his reputation and earned the respect of many people around him. Yet his personal life does not reflect the things he fought for outside of his

## PARENT'S INITIATIVE

home. He was a Levite, and that meant he was a priest. So were his sons. But his sons didn't take their responsibility seriously.

The needs of all Levites were meant to be met through the tithes of the people of Israel. This is how Eli had provided for his family, and his sons' needs were to be provided for in this manner as well. Needless to say, Eli's sons took advantage of their position to satisfy their strong desire for power, possessions, and control. In the New Living Translation Bible, this is how you are introduced to them:

> "Now the sons of Eli were scoundrels who had no respect for the Lord" (1 Samuel 2:12).

Let me remind you that they were priests, but this is how you first come to know them: scoundrels who had no respect for the Lord. The way they were living went against the standards and morals of the priesthood. They were neglecting everything the priesthood stood for as well as the guidelines they were to follow in their duties. They were taking parts of the sacrifices that were to be offered to God on the behalf of other people and eating the fat of the meat before the fat was burned off. You may be thinking, *What's the big deal? What's a little fat?* This was against God's Law. They were going against the strict process God had established for these sacrifices.

These sacrifices were considered as offerings before the Lord. Their focus was on giving God honor and respect and on being forgiven for their sins. So as these scoundrel priests were presenting these sacrifices to the Lord on behalf of the people, they were themselves sinning because they were not presenting the sacrifices as they should have. They were actually taking the parts that belonged to the Lord for themselves. Not only were they doing this, but they were also sleeping with the women who served there. This is where it gets really bad. Obviously, it's already bad that his sons were not following the procedures God had set for them, but it gets much worse when we read the next part about Eli.

## NEGLECTING AWARENESS

> "Now Eli was very old, but he was *aware* of what his sons were doing to the people of Israel" (1 Samuel 2:22, emphasis mine).

Eli knew what was going on with his sons, but he didn't do anything substantial about it. If you read a little further, all he did was yell at them. That wasn't enough. According to the law of Moses, as the high priest Eli should have sentenced his sons to death for their actions. They were acting with total disregard for the importance of what they were doing—even for the holiness of God Himself. It would be hard for any father to sentence his sons to death, but their actions affected not only them but the whole nation of Israel. Eli was aware and did very little about it. He should have taken action. What happens next takes it to the next level.

> "One day a man of God came to Eli and gave him this message from the Lord" (1 Samuel 2:27).

The message that this man brought wasn't the typical uplifting message that many of us have grown accustomed to hearing on a Sunday morning. It was a very serious rebuke. It was also a firm reminder of the importance of what Eli was called to do and the action he had failed to take. He was the high priest, and because he didn't do anything about his sons' sin, the Lord was now stepping in Himself. Eli honored his sons above God and allowed their sins to continue.

Think about it: Eli spent his whole life serving God. His overall job description was to oversee all the worship in Israel, but he couldn't even take care of his own home. He saw what was going on and did nothing about it. Being well-respected among the people of Israel mattered more to Eli than anything else. Because he did nothing, judgment fell upon himself and his family line.

### King David and His Sons, Amnon and Absalom

The Bible says that David was known as a man after God's own heart. Many of us can relate to his life story. He wasn't perfect by any

## PARENT'S INITIATIVE

means; but in the midst of his imperfections, he was still known for being a great man of God. The sin he committed that most of us are aware of is sleeping with Bathsheba (1 Samuel 11). That sin alone opened a Pandora's box in his life and that of his family. It was the beginning of a rough road for his entire family. (We need to remind ourselves on a daily basis that our personal sins don't only affect us; they affect everyone close to us as well.) From that mistake, we also become aware of another shortcoming David had. David, the man known as a man after God's own heart, fell short in being a good father as well.

It was probably hard to balance a kingdom and a family. Not only are you considered a father at home, but also a father to a nation. To top it all off, David also had several concubines, wives, and children. I am sure that on several occasions there were those in his household who felt neglected because of a lack of attention or even priority. To try to balance all those relationships would be a huge burden for anyone.

Being the son of a king would have its perks, but also its downfalls. On the one hand, you could probably have anything you wanted any time you wanted it; on the other, you might have had to compete for the attention of your father. Amnon was David's firstborn son. He was born and raised when David was making a name for himself and came into power. You would think that being the son of a king would give you a sense of entitlement and maybe a lot of time on your hands. You might have servants to do whatever you wanted at any time and have many other resources at your disposal. I would go as far as to say that I am sure all of David's kids were spoiled. When your kids are spoiled, they don't like to hear the word "no" and don't respond well when they are not allowed to have something they want.

Amnon found himself wanting his half-sister, Tamar. The Bible says that she was beautiful and Amnon was desperately in love with her. He was so in love that he became very sick because he thought he could never have her. It would be safe to say that his "love" for her was actually lust. That much becomes clear as everything unfolds. Amnon devised a scheme to seduce Tamar with the advice of his cousin, and it failed. Then he chose to rape her, but after he got what he wanted he

## NEGLECTING AWARENESS

was disgusted by her. He didn't want anything to do with her. When his brother Absalom got wind of it, he wasn't too happy about it all. Tamar was the full-blood sister of Absalom, and he wanted revenge for the disgrace Amnon had brought on his sister. Because she was no longer a virgin, she would more than likely never marry. Absalom took revenge into his own hands and had Amnon killed.

This was some serious conflict, and I think it's safe to say that it could have been avoided. When I read this story, this is what bothered me more than anything else. Don't get me wrong: I was bothered by the fact that Tamar was raped by her half-brother and discarded like she was garbage. That bothered me a lot, but what bothered me even more was the fact that *David knew about it and did nothing*. All he did was get angry. What bothers me even more is that he knew about it and did nothing *for two years*.

> "When King David heard what had happened, he was very angry. And though Absalom never spoke to Amnon about this, he hated Amnon deeply because of what he had done to his sister. Two years later ..." (2 Samuel 13:21–23).

David's family had to be huge. I am sure that what happened to Tamar was no secret. Everyone knew about it. Could you imagine this thing lingering over his family for two years? And nothing was done about it? Think about the family gatherings, birthday parties, celebrations, feasts, going to the temple as a family, and so on. All that time, everyone was wondering if and when David would address the situation. He was very well aware of it. I am sure he noticed that Amnon and Absalom were not talking. I am sure he noticed Absalom giving Amnon the "stink eye" at the family get together. The tension had to be really bad.

David was very well aware and did nothing. After two years of no action by the king, his father, Absalom devised a plan and took action himself. If I were Absalom, I would have been frustrated too. Day in and day out, you see how your father handles the affairs of his kingdom, and yet he doesn't do anything about what is going on in his own household.

# PARENT'S INITIATIVE

David neglected the issues in his own home, but I am sure he was swift to take action when it came to his kingdom. I am sure that this instance of inaction had a lot to do with Absalom's eventual rebellion against David: Absalom later slept with his father's concubines and took over the kingdom for a period of time.

There was a lot of drama in the household of King David. It was like a modern-day episode of a soap opera. The drama began with his sin with Bathsheba and then not taking action when he became *aware* of his son Amnon raping his own daughter. Who I am to say that it could have been avoided because of the judgment of his original sin? I am not sure. Only God can answer that. I do know this: David knew and took no action. All he did was get mad about it. Who is to say that Absalom would have handled it differently had David done something? Only God knows.

## My Take on These Two Unfortunate Events

When it comes to these two examples, there is one thing that really bothers me. Eli, the high priest of Israel and in his own home, didn't take serious action. David, king of Israel and ultimately king of his own home, didn't take action. That lack of action made it seem like they both were okay with sin. I am sure a lot of people knew about the actions of their sons, and it probably seemed like it was "okay" because neither authority did anything. It was their responsibility to do something about it. They were responsible not only for protecting their own homes, but the "home" of the Lord as well.

I look at it this way, and I think we can find some common ground here: Parents are the high priests of their homes and oversee them. Our home is our sanctuary. When something is wrong in our home, that is not good and we are to do something about it, especially when we are made aware of it. Action needs to be taken because the problem will not only affect one individual—it will affect everyone. There is a lot of turmoil in homes because parents are not dealing with problems. They are aware of them but don't want to deal with them.

## NEGLECTING AWARENESS

It could be a rebellious teen who has no regard for the rules that have been set and continues to break them. When nothing is done about it, that lack of action will teach them that they don't have to follow the rules. Not only will they not follow the rules at home, but eventually they will not follow them at school or society at large. Then, in turn, any younger siblings in the home will do the same because of the model that is set before them. No action for the one snowballs to the rest. It will be an endless cycle until they all leave the home.

How about the parents who know their daughter is sleeping around and do nothing about it? She may become pregnant, which isn't the worst thing that could happen to her, but she could also acquire an STD that would be with her the rest of her life. This STD could keep her from having babies in the future and may not be noticed for up to six years. On top of that, she will have a great deal of emotional baggage to handle in the future, as will a sexually active boy. I could give example after example, but I don't think it's necessary. I am sure there are many that you could think of too; you may even have faced your own issues recently.

The key thing is: If you are aware of something that is taking place in your home, you need to do something about it. It is up to you to take the initiative and make changes that are necessary. You can see what took place in the home of these two men and the destruction that came from it. You may have never heard the story of Eli and his sons, but most people know of David. Once again, he was known as a man after God's own heart and yet still experienced terrible conflict in his own home. If only these men would have done what was needed; it would have saved some heartache, not only for themselves but everyone in their family.

Read this carefully: It's not always easy taking action, but as the leaders of our homes, we need to lead our families to their promised land. God has great things in store for everyone in your household. Not just for your children, but for you as well. When we make it a priority to honor God in everything we do, He will in turn take care of us and will be with us every step of the way. We will have some difficult times, but I believe they will not be as frequent if we do what we need to do,

## PARENT'S INITIATIVE

especially when we are made aware. Stop neglecting the truth and take the initiative.

### Application Questions for Chapter 12

1. In what ways have you neglected awareness in your home? If so, what are you doing to address it?
2. Can you relate to the story of Eli and his sons? If so, how? Are you taking steps to make it better?
3. Can you relate to the story of Amnon and David? If so, how? Are you taking steps to make it better?
4. Are you willing to allow the Holy Spirit to speak to you about neglect? Would you commit to being more open and willing to hear and obey Him as He makes you aware of things?
5. ACTION STEP: Have you already neglected something that you saw as you read this book? If so, what? What action steps need to be taken to address that neglect?

# Chapter 13: Encouragement

"Because you are my helper, I sing for joy in the shadow of your wings. I cling to you; your strong right hand holds me securely" (Psalm 63:7–8).

I am hoping that by now you have already begun to make some changes. You have been made aware of some things and are taking the initiative to make the necessary improvements. It is a process, and it is going to take time to see improvement. There are times when we can see instant change and other times when change seems to be taking forever. I am not one for change unless it is really necessary. I prefer change that takes time and work; and I would like to think that this type of change is deeper, more appreciated, and has the tendency to stick more. Slow change allows you to make adjustments and reinforce what needs to be reinforced. Slow change tends to stick more than the quick change because that can be easily forgotten.

You are probably going to face some resistance from your children as you make changes; it may even come from your spouse as well. There are those who will think you may be a little too extreme in the way you choose to live your life and raise your kids. Even those close to you who do not comprehend the responsibility that has been placed on you as a parent may not understand. People who are not living for the Lord will definitely not understand. That is why the Bible stresses that we are not to do things as they do.

## PARENT'S INITIATIVE

"'I will live in them and walk among them. I will be their God, and they will be my people. Therefore, come out from among unbelievers, and separate yourselves from them, says the Lord'" (2 Corinthians 6:16–17).

"For you are a holy people, who belong to the Lord your God. Of all the people on earth, the Lord your God has chosen you to be his own special treasure" (Deuteronomy 7:6).

It is all about Him and what He wants to do through you and your family. We succeed when we make it all about Him. He wants to live among us. He does not want us to be like the unbelievers of this world. When we choose to parent as God has called us to parent, we are going to separate ourselves and people are not going to understand. It has been said that when you are facing opposition and even criticism, you are more than likely doing something right. To choose His way is to set yourself up as His own special treasure.

I know that it is easier said than done. When I speak with people, I stress that because I know that is so true. I can sit there and counsel people as they are going through a difficult time, and I can say all the right things, but it is one thing to speak and another to do it and live through it. There are those who have been through a living hell in their homes because of the actions of their kids and the consequences that came with them. I want to say that there is hope and that I can say this in confidence:

"So be strong and courageous! Do not be afraid and do not panic before them. For the Lord your God will personally go ahead of you. He will neither fail you nor abandon you" (Deuteronomy 31:6).

These words were given by Moses to Israel before Joshua became their leader. These words apply to us, too, in every area of our lives. As we become aware of things in our homes and even in our own

## ENCOURAGEMENT

personal lives, we need to be strong and courageous. We do not need to be afraid to address our problems; the worst thing we can do is panic. God is going before us as we live our lives for Him, and He will never fail us or abandon us. Things may not always go our way, and I am sure that we can think of a better course than the one that unfolded for us sometimes. Our primary responsibility is to continue to move forward and trust in Him. One thing that we have a tendency to forget is the fact that *God is in this with us*.

> "For we are co-workers in God's service; you are God's field, God's building" (1 Corinthians 3:9 NIV).

We are in this together with God. He does not leave us to ourselves. He is with us and working alongside us. The key is that we allow Him to join us and are not trying to do it on our own. That is the problem that a lot of people have because they don't want to involve God, or think He is too busy to get involved. We are in this with Him and He wants to use us and help us to mold us and our family into His image. You are His field and His building. As you give Him access, He will help you plant, water, till the ground, and take care of the maintenance (or upkeep). It comes down to us allowing Him to have His way in our lives and in our homes, and making the necessary changes and sacrifices, so that He can reside in our homes and lives.

I want to share one more story from the Bible. It is a great way to sum up everything in this book and the responsibility that we have as parents. The story of Hannah has to be one of my favorites. She could not have any children, and to be barren in this time was a reproach. She was taunted by her husband's other wife because she, unlike Hannah, was able to bear children. Every year they went to offer sacrifices as a family at the temple. What was supposed to be a time of worship and sacrifice unto the Lord was a bitter reminder to Hannah of her barren state.

The Bible said that each time, she was reduced to tears and would not even eat. Can you imagine that? How difficult that had to be for

## PARENT'S INITIATIVE

Hannah. To share your husband with someone who is able to bear children and enjoy the fruit of it and be taunted every year at a time of worship and sacrifice. Her husband tried to console her, but to no avail.

Hannah finally got fed up and did what she should have done before: she prayed at the temple. I love the way the Bible says that she found herself in deep anguish, crying bitterly as she prayed to the Lord. She went on to make a vow to the Lord. She asked that He would look upon her and give her a son. Once this son was given to her, she would, in turn, give him back to the Lord. She said that he would be the Lord's for his entire life, and as a sign that he has been dedicated to the Lord, his hair would never be cut.

She went on to have a small encounter with the priest that you may now be familiar with: Eli. He accused her of being drunk because he was watching her pray, and she had only been moving her lips and not praying aloud. Of course, she denied that she was drunk and went on to tell Eli that she was discouraged and pouring her heart out to the Lord. Eli told her to go in peace and prayed that her request be granted. I love what happened next! She went back and began to eat, and she was no longer sad! The *whole* family got up the next morning and went to worship the Lord.

It was like something finally clicked in her. She finally became *aware* of the fact that she had never talked to the Lord about her condition. Year after year, she had been taunted by the woman that she shared her husband. The Lord was obviously aware of her condition, but was waiting on her to take the initiative. She really took action when she went to the temple and cried out to God. He gave her a renewed confidence because she placed her problem in the hands of God. She got her child and she did what she had vowed to do. Some time after weaning her son, she dropped him off at the temple to serve the Lord for the rest of his life. Her son, the prophet Samuel, was an awesome man of God and officially the last judge of Israel.

There are a couple of things I want to encourage you with through this story. As parents, we need to realize that our children are a gift from God, as Hannah did, and then dedicate them to the service of

## ENCOURAGEMENT

the Lord. Obviously, we cannot drop them off at the local church at a very young age, but we can pray for them and offer them a home that honors God. We must give them a home that truly been given over to God, to which He has access, and in which He is allowed to rule and reign. It should be a home that is not full of compromise, but makes the Lord a priority instead. We must create safe harbors that teach the ways of the Lord and allow our children the opportunity to grow and be dedicated to the Lord for the rest of their lives.

We need to pray as Hannah did for our kids. She prayed hard and then went on with her business as though the Lord had already met her request. She did her part and trusted the Lord was going to do His. That is the way we need to go about it as well. You may find yourself going through hell in your home; you are very well aware. Take the initiative and pray in deep anguish, crying out to the Lord. Know that He hears your prayer, and take action. Do what you can to be the parent you are called to be and leave it in His hands. If everything is going well in your home, do what you can to keep it that way; continue to pray and trust in God for the best for your children. When you are made aware of something, take the initiative to make improvements.

Always remember that we are in this together and you are not alone. Don't try to do this on your own. There are several other people who God has strategically placed in your life that are there to help you. These people are also parents and may be going through the same things you are dealing with—perhaps they have even found a way to deal with it. If anything, they could become prayer partners. Ultimately, we are all family, and we need to be there for one another and fight for one another.

> "Just as our bodies have many parts and each part has a special function, so it is with Christ's body. We are many parts of one body, and we all belong to each other" (Romans 12:4–5).

## PARENT'S INITIATIVE

May the *Parent's Initiative* become a movement and not just another fad. May parents become the parents they are called to be and take the responsibility that God has placed on their lives seriously. May we join together as one body and function as God has called us to.

May we no longer be so *passive* and allow things to continue that need to be dealt with. May we find a healthy balance in areas in which we may be too *aggressive* that, in turn, may cause our children to rebel. May we work on the *relationships* that God has blessed us with on a daily basis and be more careful in the way we allow *entertainment* to influence our homes and ourselves. May we deal with *nonsense* and, with the *training* that God has given, may we talk to and educate our kids about *sex* as much as we can, so that they may enjoy it with the spouse God has specifically set aside for them. Finally*, let us not neglect the awareness* that God at all times will allow us to see in our homes and even in our own personal lives. May we take action before it is too late. May we always reflect on how our lives and our homes may not be honoring God! May we always be *encouraged* in Him and not allow this world to discourage us.

We are in this together! I pray that this will help you become even more *aware* and that you will take the *initiative*. I do not have all the answers as a parent, but it is my prayer that this book has made you more aware of what is going on in your own home and life so you may trust in God to help you find ways to take the initiative in finding the solutions to address your problems. God is with you, and He will never forsake you. He is walking ahead of you, and it is up to you to trust in Him and give Him access.

Once again, let us come together and not only pray for our children and our homes, but also for parents all over this world. This is a call on our lives and a gift that God has blessed us with! Let us be good stewards and dedicate our children to the Lord for His service, as we do what we can to provide that avenue for Him to have His way in every way possible! Blessing upon you, your family, and your home!

# ENCOURAGEMENT

## Application Questions for Chapter 13

1. How are you further equipping yourself personally to grow and mature as a parent? If not, what are some things you can do?
2. Can you relate to Hannah? If so, how? What could you do or not do to be like Hannah?
3. Would you take the time now to follow us on social media to receive further encouragement, challenges, or just to be a part of a community of people that are in this together? If so, do it right now. Simply search for "Parent's Initiative" on Facebook, Instagram, and YouTube.
4. ACTION STEP: Do you intentionally spend time in prayer specifically for fulfilling your role as a parent? If not, would you commit to do so now? Would you be willing to write out specific prayers and pray them?